COMPREHENSIVE RESEARCH
AND STUDY GUIDE

BLOOM'S MAJOR SHORT STORY WRITERS

John *Cheever*

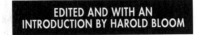

EDITED AND WITH AN
INTRODUCTION BY HAROLD BLOOM

CURRENTLY AVAILABLE

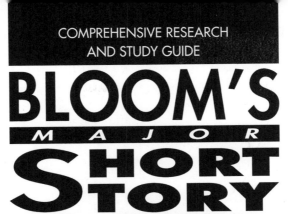

COMPREHENSIVE RESEARCH
AND STUDY GUIDE

BLOOM'S
MAJOR
SHORT
STORY
WRITERS

John
Cheever

CHELSEA HOUSE
PUBLISHERS
A Haights Cross Communications Company

Philadelphia

Printed and bound in the United States of America.

First Printing
1 3 5 7 9 8 6 4 2

Library of Congress Cataloging-in-Publication Data

John Cheever / edited and with an introduction by Harold Bloom.
    p. cm. — (Bloom's Major Short Story Writers)
  Includes bibliographical references and index.
  ISBN 0-7910-7589-3
  1. Cheever, John—Criticism and interpretation. 2. Short story.
I. Bloom, Harold. II. Series.
  PS3505.H6428 Z7 2003
  813'.52—dc22

                                                    2003019992

Chelsea House Publishers
1974 Sproul Road, Suite 400
Broomall, PA 19008-0914

3 1559 00158 6997

www.chelseahouse.com

Contributing Editor: Mei Chin

Cover design by Terry Mallon

Layout by EJB Publishing Services

CONTENTS

USER'S GUIDE

This volume is designed to present biographical, critical, and bibliographical information on the author and the author's best-known or most important short stories. Following Harold Bloom's editor's note and introduction is a concise biography of the author that discusses major life events and important literary accomplishments. A critical analysis of each story follows, tracing significant themes, patterns, and motifs in the work. An annotated list of characters supplies brief information on the main characters in each story.

A selection of critical extracts, derived from previously published material, follows each thematic analysis. In most cases, these extracts represent the best analysis available from a number of leading critics. Because these extracts are derived from previously published material, they will include the original notations and references when available. Each extract is cited, and readers are encouraged to use the original publications as they continue their research. A bibliography of the author's writings, a list of additional books and articles on the author and their work, and an index of themes and ideas conclude the volume.

As with any study guide, this volume is designed as a supplement to the works being discussed, and is in no way intended as a replacement for those works. The reader is advised to read the text prior to using this study guide, and to keep it accessible for quick reference.

ABOUT THE EDITOR

Harold Bloom is Sterling Professor of the Humanities at Yale University and Henry W. and Albert A. Berg Professor of English at the New York University Graduate School. He is the author of over 20 books, and the editor of more than 30 anthologies of literary criticism.

Professor Bloom's works include *Shelley's Mythmaking* (1959), *The Visionary Company* (1961), *Blake's Apocalypse* (1963), *Yeats* (1970), *A Map of Misreading* (1975), *Kabbalah and Criticism* (1975), *Agon: Toward a Theory of Revisionism* (1982), *The American Religion* (1992), *The Western Canon* (1994), and *Omens of Millennium: The Gnosis of Angels, Dreams, and Resurrection* (1996). *The Anxiety of Influence* (1973) sets forth Professor Bloom's provocative theory of the literary relationships between the great writers and their predecessors. His most recent books include *Shakespeare: The Invention of the Human*, a 1998 National Book Award finalist, *How to Read and Why* (2000), *Genius: A Mosaic of One Hundred Exemplary Creative Minds* (2002), and *Hamlet: Poem Unlimited* (2003).

Professor Bloom earned his Ph.D. from Yale University in 1955 and has served on the Yale faculty since then. He is a 1985 MacArthur Foundation Award recipient and served as the Charles Eliot Norton Professor of Poetry at Harvard University in 1987–88. In 1999 he was awarded the prestigious American Academy of Arts and Letters Gold Medal for Criticism. Professor Bloom is the editor of several other Chelsea House series in literary criticism, including BLOOM'S MAJOR SHORT STORY WRITERS, BLOOM'S MAJOR NOVELISTS, BLOOM'S MAJOR DRAMATISTS, BLOOM'S MODERN CRITICAL INTERPRETATIONS, BLOOM'S MODERN CRITICAL VIEWS, BLOOM'S BIOCRITIQUES, BLOOM'S GUIDES, BLOOM'S MAJOR LITERARY CHARACTERS, and BLOOM'S PERIOD STUDIES.

EDITOR'S NOTE

This volume offers critical views of five stories by John Cheever, all of them permanent achievements.

My Introduction interprets "The Country Husband," which I regard as Cheever's masterpiece.

"Goodbye, My Brother" is illuminated by Cheever's own account of the story's origins, while "The Enormous Radio," probably the most famous of Cheever's tales, is shrewdly read by James E. O'Hara as a fantastic allegory in which Cheever himself *is* the radio.

Patrick Meanor sensitively traces Cheever's ironic parodies of the English poet and visionary William Blake in the sadistic splendor of Cheever's "The Five-Forty-Eight."

For Lawrence Jay Dessner, "The Country Husband" allows Mrs. Weed little sympathy, a judgment a little at variance with my experience of the story.

"The Swimmer," another of Cheever's strong battles against the influence of Scott Fitzgerald, is darkly impressive in Nathan Cervo's unpacking of its allusive images of Hades, out of which Merrill has emerged, an earthbound shade.

INTRODUCTION
Harold Bloom

I join the many readers unable to abandon a perpetual return to John Cheever's "The Country Husband" (1955). One cannot quite name Cheever as one of the modern American story-writers of the highest eminence: Hemingway, Faulkner, Willa Cather, Katherine Anne Porter, Scott Fitzgerald, Eudora Welty, Flannery O'Conner. Still, Cheever compares favorably enough with the second order: Sherwood Anderson, Nabokov, Malamud, Updike, Ozick, Ann Beattie, Carver, and the Canadian Alice Munro. Like them, he lacks the enduring originality of Hemingway and Faulkner, but Cheever is as assured and finished as Nabokov or Updike.

"The Country Husband" disturbs me intensely with each rereading, even if it is less universal a vision of failed marriage than clearly it intends to be. Francis Weed is no Everyman, even though I have encountered (and taught) many of his potential doubles. Aesthetically, Cheever's story gains more than it loses by a certain forlorn inner solitude in Weed, who sometimes suggests a misplaced writer, like Cheever himself.

Where does one locate the haunting splendor of "The Country Husband?" Not, I think, in the idea of order that will keep the Weeds together until death, dubious as their love is for one another. Francis Weed's authentic desire hardly is for the baby-sitter, but for the image in his memory of the Norman young woman, shorn and stripped as punishment, with "some invaluable grandeur in her nakedness." A superb artist, John Cheever lacquers his surfaces, but the dark power of his best stories' undersong is their reliance upon the deviance of the sexual drive into sado-masochism.

BIOGRAPHY OF

John Cheever

John Cheever, one of twentieth century America's most distinctive chroniclers and a master short story writer, was many things: a liar, an alcoholic, and an adulterer; the progeny of a charming, financially inept Yankee father of good colonial stock and a pragmatic English mother who occupied herself with good works; a testament to both a chilly Massachusetts childhood and a sophisticated suburban upbringing. Born on May 27, 1912 in Quincy, Massachusetts, John Cheever was an unwanted child. His father, Frederick Lincoln Cheever, was head of a shoe factory but lost his job in 1926; his mother, Mary "Liley" Cheever, was an able businesswoman and organizer who started two businesses—a dress shop and gift shop—during the years her husband was unable to find work. They would later separate. Though his parents were preoccupied with economic difficulties, they did introduce him to such writers as Charles Dickens and Jack London. Cheever, who had difficulty with his mother's businesslike manner and father's alcoholism, turned to his less prosaic family members for inspiration—notably an ancestral cousin by the name of Ezekiel Cheever who was a seventeenth century schoolmaster, royal dissident, and philosopher.

From the time he was very young, Cheever wanted to be a writer, and, with this goal in mind, was academically delinquent in everything else. In 1930, after being asked to leave the prestigious Thayer Academy, he penned "Expelled," a precocious, admittedly self-indulgent, quasi-autobiographical narrative that appeared in the *New Republic* and turned him into an overnight adolescent sensation. Ironically, this future winner of the Pulitzer Prize and National Book Award never completed high school. On the heels of his first success, Cheever moved to Boston to live with his older brother Fred, and the seven years that separated them proved insignificant. The two siblings were close and the result was one of alternating affection and suffocation that would follow Cheever for the rest of his life, expressed in his writing most often as fratricide. ("I killed you off in *Falconer*," he reportedly said to Fred the year Fred died. "Oh good…" Fred replied, "you've been trying all these years."[1])

Cheever moved to New York in 1932 on the advice of E.E. Cummings, following in the footsteps of the talented young New York writers before him. He managed an invitation to the Yaddo mansion, an elite artist's colony that boasted such visitors as Katherine Ann Porter and Truman Capote, and a published story in *The New Yorker*. Both institutions would become permanent fixtures in his life, and he would contribute over 100 stories to *The New Yorker* in his lifetime. In 1941, he met and married Mary Winsternez. She had stellar pedigree that nice upper middle class boys like John Cheever yearned for—the daughter of the dean of Yale studies and the stepdaughter of a Peabody. She was a graduate of Sarah Lawrence, a talented teacher and a poet who crafted several poems that have stood on their own merits. Cheever was fond of pointing out that, as a reader, she was never his greatest fan. She was bright, beautiful, and somewhat rigid. Theirs was a marriage that began in a smitten springtime fervor, produced three children, and would eventually last through numerous betrayals, a major separation, and repeated threats of divorce. Its success was due in part because Cheever, in his heart of hearts, was a family man, and in part because the two shared "humor." "….[P]eople named John and Mary," he wrote in his novel *Bullet Park*, "never divorced."

The young Cheevers took up residence with two other couples in a townhouse located on 92nd street in New York, and their subsequent social escapades were fodder for his quaint, Noel Coward-esque, and generally forgotten "Townhouse Stories." The couple had three children: Susan in 1943, Benjamin in 1948, and Federico in 1957. Susan and Benjamin would both become authors. Meanwhile, Cheever had been drafted to the army, but was transferred at the last minute to the role of reporter—mercifully, it seems now, considering that his regiment suffered some of the most devastating losses of D-Day. After the war, the Cheevers transferred to Sutton Place (another popular Cheever location) and then to the suburbs—first Scarborough, and then Ossining—which would provide him with enough material for the rest of his writing career. There were also stints in Rome and Russia. He published his first novel, *The Wapshot Chronicle*, in 1957.

With the first *Wapshot* novel and the stories he was composing at the same time, Cheever began to create neighborhoods that he would build on for the years to come—St. Boltophs (of the *Wapshot* series), Bullet Park, and Shady Hill of the short stories. The result is a curious intimacy that develops between character and reader. When Mr. Hammer murders his neighbor's son in *Bullet Park*, we think wistfully of his waterlogged neighbor Neddy Merrill in "The Swimmer"; when Francis Weed chats to Trace Bearden on the train in "The Country Husband," we remember Bearden's best friend Cash Bentley, whose ill-fated end was documented in "O Youth and Beauty." We recognize other names, less well defined—the Facquarsons, the Trenchers, Mr. TK who is the Shady Hill stationmaster, and the elderly Mrs. Heinlein who babysits the Shady Hill children. In short, these characters continue to exist long after a story has ended, and to encounter them later is to feel the same joy we might experience when we encounter a friend from our playground days.

As he built his fiction repertoire, Cheever also began to drink. "I chain smoke, I chain drink, I chain everything else," he told Leslie Aldridge at the St. Regis Hotel in 1969.[2] His father had been an alcoholic; his brother, Fred had battled drinking several times and failed, and it was only when John Cheever was faced with the possibility of dying in a squalid apartment in Boston, separated from his family, that he quit. (Funnily enough, while Cheever's prose and alcohol are inexorably entangled, Cheever rarely writes about its demons; his characters drink and that is all.) He also had a restless appetite for both women and for men, and could count the actress Hope Lange and the writer Max Zimmer among his conquests. As an artist, however, he was modest and the most generous of men. One can only point to the affection with which he nurtured his students (Allan Gurganus among them) and the regard with which he held his colleagues (Saul Bellow, Norman Mailer, and John Updike, with whom he went to Russia). "Writing is not at all a competitive sport," he famously declared to his daughter Susan in 1977.[3] He was also a loving father, and whether or not he was always a good one, his children Susan and Ben both affirm that the intention was always there. Just like his characters, then, Cheever was not a perfect man, yet he was a decent one, who believed in heroism and sentiment and family and a minor man's capacity to glory.

As much as he loved drink, quitting alcohol in 1975 gave Cheever a new life. He taught literature at the nearby prison Sing Sing, started a lasting friendship with the inmate Donald Lang, and later channeled his experiences into the novel, *Falconer* (1977), which was quite a departure from his well bred milieu. He won the Pulitzer Prize for his *Collected Stories* in 1979. When Cheever was diagnosed with the terminal cancer that would take his life in 1981, his longtime lover Max Zimmer regularly took a train from the city and then returned with Cheever and the family car for treatments at Sloan-Kettering. They would then drive back to Ossining where Mary Cheever would have supper waiting. It was a dying worthy of Cheever's imagination— elegant, absurd, radiant, and above all, civil.

NOTES

1. Scott Donaldson, ed. *John Cheever: A Biography*. New York: Random House, 1988: p. 301.

2. Leslie Aldridge, "Having a Drink with Cheever," in *Conversations with John Cheever*, ed. Scott Donaldson (Jackson: University Press of Mississipi, 1987): p. 37.

3. Susan Cheever Cowley, "A Duet of Cheevers," in *Conversations with John Cheever*, ed. Scott Donaldson (Jackson: University Press of Mississipi, 1987): p. 128.

"Goodbye, My Brother"

Cheever never considered the compilation of his short stories to be a major feat; indeed, he would not have collected them had it not been for the persuasion of editor Bob Gottlieb, and in the end, all he claimed he did "was pull stories from under the bed."[1] But in its organization, *The Short Stories of John Cheever* (1977) betrays mastery and careful planning. That Cheever chose to lead with the 1951 story "Goodbye, My Brother," even though it post-dates several other stories, means that he was aware of the importance of a seductive start.

"Goodbye, My Brother" is a grand story, far more skillful than many of the later works. More importantly, however, there is no other story that is more intrinsically representative of its author, or more personal. The personal aspect is immediately evident in its use of first person, a technique that Cheever rarely deploys. The backdrop and events are both typical of his writing and redolent with Cheever's own memories, as his comments on the drafting of the story affirm (see the excerpt "What Happened"). There is the house on the Massachussetts coast; as well as the endless evenings of backgammon, gin, and club dances. There is the motif of brother against brother. But there is also the struggle that is fundamental to all of Cheever—that of the pagan man who loves a decadent, deluded life, and that of the writer who cannot help but see through it.

The premise is simple enough. The Pommeroy clan—the family matriarch and the grown siblings Diana, Chaddy, and the narrator, along with their families—gather at their house on the Massachusetts shore, as they have done every summer, only this time, for the first time in years, their estranged younger brother Lawrence joins them. Lawrence is a disapproving, puritanical man, and as soon as he arrives, he seems intent on spoiling the usual Pommeroy fun. He abuses the house (it will wash away in the sea, he complains, it is a new house that has wasted thousands of dollars to make itself look old), lobbies the cook to join a union, and refuses to participate in the usual activities of tennis, backgammon, drinking martinis, and swimming at the beach. When the local club gives a costume dance, Lawrence and his wife Ruth appear in ordinary clothes. Finally, outraged, the narrator hits Lawrence on the head with a tree root and Lawrence collapses on the sand, bleeding. By the next morning, Lawrence has departed, and the narrator is left to his own ruminations, and to the glorious sight of his wife and his sister emerging out of the water: "I saw they were naked, unshy, beautiful, and full of grace, and I watched the naked women walk out of the sea."

The story is at its most basic a marvelous reimagining of Cain and Abel. Lawrence Pommeroy is a good man; he has spent his life pursuing right even when it puts him at the risk of alienating others; his sister Diana calls him "Little Jesus." The rest of the Pommeroys, in contrast, are silly, decadent, usually and even perhaps a little heartless. Pommeroy women personify pagan sensuality, and have been christened with names to match—the narrator's wife Helen, with her dyed golden hair, recalls Helen of Troy; coquettish Odette, Chaddy's wife, echoes the seductress in *Swann's Way;* divorced sister Diana is just as ruthless as the Roman goddess to whom she owes her name. Nothing represents the Pommeroy willingness to self-delusion better than their attitude at their drowned father's funeral—the "ceremony and decorum" of answering "mannerly condolences with mannerly grief." Unpleasantness in the Pommeroy household is soothed by pretty ritual. Therefore, "drinking straight rum or bringing a beer can to the dinner table" can cause insurmountable conflict, for the distortion of such niceties threatens to expose the unease that such niceties are supposed to disguise.

The Pommeroys also like to swim. Swimming has often been used as a symbol for sacred cleansing, but in Cheever, a dip in the water is more complex, for the purification it offers is merely temporary. It is, in the end, a futile attempt to put our stains behind, just as Neddy Merrill will try later in "The Swimmer." At the end of the costume party, middle-aged men in high school football uniforms jump in the pool, a symbolic denial of their age. The family, after the first upsetting night with Lawrence, go "swimming in the dark." Pommeroys swim for the same reasons that they drink—for the obscurity it offers.

The Pommeroys are not clever. When Lawrence attacks their characters, no one can come up with a satisfying rejoinder. The family's only defense is to pretend that he doesn't exist. "Let's have a fabulous morning," they say, or, "I don't mind *him*." The primary target of his wrath—Mother—gets drunk the night of his arrival. In the family, Lawrence is the only one who enjoys success—he is a lawyer, in contrast to the narrator, who is a mediocre schoolteacher who quarters his family in a school-run residence, eats school dinners, and has no hope of being headmaster. But even professional failure cannot compare to the narrator's lack of insight. "You're a fool," Lawrence accuses the narrator, and Lawrence is right. The narrator blames Lawrence's pessimism as "an unwillingness to grasp realities." And in Lawrence's response, we sense just how outrageously off-mark the narrator is: "What are the realities? Diana is a foolish and promiscuous woman. Mother is an alcoholic ... Chaddy is dishonest ...The house is going to fall into the sea." To answer, the narrator calls Lawrence a "gloomy son of a bitch," words that are reminiscent of the empty insults slung in schoolyard fights. In the end, like a teenage bully, the only way he can avenge himself is by resorting to violence.

But Laurence/Abel's virtue makes him a miserable person. We sympathize with the Pommeroys, because, in Cheever's opinion, one cannot do wrong unless one is aware of the wrong itself. Hence, the Pommeroys' blindness makes them inculpable. Buzzed on martinis and oversexed, they are strangely free of sin; theirs is an Eden of gin and cigarettes and plunging necklines. Lawrence, with his intellect and virtue, serves only to cast gloom; not only he, but his wife and children suffer from his Puritan, joyless view. Obsessed with the world's wrongs, he is incapable of ever seeing any beauty. His is the "eye in the crowd ... seeking out the cheek with acne, the infirm hand." He cannot look at the sea without thinking of the war in Spain and his father's unfound body. On the other hand, his family, who love the sea simply because it is "iridescent and dark," want no more than to spread gladness.

It is no mistake that "Pommeroy" derives from the French words *pommes* and *roi*. Essentially, the Pommeroys are the Kings of the Apples, apples being Cheever's favorite fruit, Eden's fruit of knowledge.[2] But while the Pommeroys may guard over the fruit of knowledge, they do not eat it. Lawrence, on the other hand, has bitten and is full of gall. "Oh, what can you do with a man like that?" mourns the narrator. In many ways hitting Lawrence seems to be the only solution. Perhaps the narrator hopes to be a catalyst for Lawrence's rebirth, that the Lawrence sprawled on the sand with a wound on his head will die and a different Lawrence will resurrect himself.

Cheever himself asserts that the dramatic tension of "Goodbye, My Brother" is a result of a personal division. In "What Happened," an essay about the background to the story, he tells us that Lawrence's observations—about backgammon, about the masquerade ball, and especially about the house with its two-hundred-year-old shingles—are lifted from his own journal. At the time, he had been staying at a friend's expensively antiquated modern house on Martha's Vineyard and, as he says, "I linked this crude sense of the past with my friend's failure to mature. The failure was national ... We failed to mature as a people and had turned back to dwell on old football triumphs, raftered ceilings, candlights, and fires."[3] But when Cheever reread these bleak observations at a later date, he did so in the spirit of a very different man, in love with the landscape and the beauty of the afternoon. On that day these two Cheevers emerged as the characters of Lawrence Pommoroy and his unnamed brother.

The split is apparent in the narrative voice. Though Cheever himself insists on his narrator's stupidity, the narrator is able to recall Lawrence's thoughts with an uncharacteristic keenness. For instance, there is a costume ball, where at least three men have dressed as football players and at least ten women have dressed as brides. This tableau infects the narrator with joy, for he sees it as clever, romantic, and a part of the most beautiful coincidence. But he is also able to comment on Lawrence's analysis:

> ... [It was] an abuse and a distortion of time; as if
> wanting to be brides and football players we exposed the
> fact that, the lights of youth having been put out in us,
> we had been unable to find other lights to go by....

Lawrence's perception, as the reader is well aware, is by far the more accurate. Ten brides and three football players are indicative of a lack of personal originality, as well as a gratuitous display of the failures of middle-age. In this skipping back and forth between the brothers, Cheever the author is able to maintain the narrator's fatuous quality all the while deftly dissecting it.

The split is even more dramatic during backgammon evening, where the narrator observes—by again assuming the thoughts of Lawrence—that virtue, self-esteem, and soul are successively gambled away. The astuteness with which he exposes his mother astonishes us with its cruelty.

> ...[S]he seems at times to be trying to divine in Chaddy
> some grief, some loss, that she can succor and redress,
> and so reestablish the relationship that she enjoyed with
> him when he was sickly and young. She loves defending
> the weak and the childlike...

Granted, this is not the narrator's opinion, this is the opinion that the narrator presumes upon Lawrence. But since these perceptions of Lawrence are in fact the narrator's own invention, they are latent in the narrator himself.

Such indeterminacy makes it easy to see why alternating points of view within a first person narrative is a technique frequently fated to failure. Cheever veers just short of this; indeed, the stylish bravura in "Goodbye, My Brother" is due to its riskiness, and is not used in the same way in any subsequent Cheever story. The narrator will find himself reincarnated in many future characters, all of them earnest, self-deluded men, but he is never allowed again to assume the story's control. The voice that narrates the other stories is a return to the man that had existed before Lawrence's inception—that is to say someone who integrates both the pessimistic and the easily pleased. Throughout the rest of his work, Cheever will struggle with his Lawrence. And while it is Cheever as a happy man, as a fool, who will lend his voice compassion and, above all, the ability to communicate a delight in life's surface beauties, it will be the clear-eyed Lawrence aspect of himself that will provide the bite, as well as the doom.

NOTES

1. Donaldson, Scott, ed. *John Cheever: A Biography*. New York: Random House, 1988: p. 321.

2. Patrick Meanor. *John Cheever Revisited*. Boston: Twayne Publishers, 1995: p. 44.

3. John Cheever, "What Happened," in *Understanding Fiction*, ed. Cleanth Brooks and Robert Penn Warren (New York: Appelton-Century-Crofts, 1959): p. 571.

"Goodbye, My Brother"

The Narrator is the second son of the Pommeroy family, a proud New England clan given to the pleasures of drinking, backgammon, swimming, and tennis during their annual two weeks at the summer house on the Massachusetts shore. A schoolteacher with no hope of being made a headmaster, he is a weak and petty man, as his brother Lawrence calls him, "a fool." Though he does not agree with his younger brother Lawrence's dour assessment of the family's excessive lifestyle, he does have an acute sense of Lawrence's judgments. Unable to resolve their differences, the narrator hits his brother over the head in a modern day Cain and Abel episode, not killing him but giving him an excuse to leave the family forever.

Lawrence is the youngest of the Pommeroy siblings, and is often referred to by his childhood nicknames of "Tifty" and "Little Jesus." Not one of the excessive Pommeroys particularly likes this brother, and Lawrence, in turn, has scorned them by becoming a lawyer, devoting his life to practical pursuits, and residing in the Midwest. His attendance at the annual Pommeroy gathering is the first in years. He is moral, pessimistic, and clever—a man whose sensibilities are attuned to the moral decay he sees in every person and situation.

Chaddy is the oldest Pommeroy son and his mother's favorite. He is the cleverest at games and sport—he wins at tennis and backgammon, but outside of this talent, he seems to nurture few other ambitions. Between himself and the narrator, there is a friendly rivalry, because they are closest in years. Lawrence calls Chaddy "dishonest."

Diana is the only Pommeroy sister, divorced and living in France, having sent her two children to boarding school in Switzerland. Lawrence frequently accuses her of promiscuity, and indeed, it is implied that her current lover is staying at an inn nearby.

Mother is a widow, once beautiful, still elegant, who enjoys propriety at the dinner table and winning at games. She also has a tendency to drink heavily, and there are glimpses of her pathetic, manipulative, and petulant character. Her favorite child is Chaddy. She loves "defending the weak and childlike," in part, perhaps, because they are the ones over whom her power is assured.

Helen has been married to the narrator for over a decade. She seems to be content with her husband's character and his lack of ambition, and she has dyed golden hair and a faded allure. When her husband attends the costume ball in his football uniform, she attends in her bridal gown, a decision that essentially declares that they are still glamorous young lovers after all.

Odette, Chaddy's wife, is a beauty with black hair and a creamy complexion that she preserves from the sunlight. She is a natural coquette, which, in Lawrence's judgment, means she is loose. When she is defeated by the narrator at backgammon, she playfully proposes that they go down into the sand dunes "to settle the score."

Ruth, Lawrence's wife, is a plain, thin woman, who declines all offers to swim with the Pommeroys, instead staying inside to do laundry in the cramped washroom with her children hovered around her.

Anna Ostrovick is the Polish cook hired for the summer at the Pommeroy's beach house, whose prime joy is to have her food eaten and appreciated. Aghast as what he deems unfair pay, Lawrence tells her she should join a union and receive benefits. Offended by his meddling, Anna tells the narrator she will leave if he doesn't stop going into "her" kitchen, and states that she is "as good as anybody."

"Goodbye, My Brother"

JOHN CHEEVER ON THE GENESIS OF THE STORY

[In the following excerpt, John Cheever explains how he appropriated observations from his own journal to create the character of Lawrence Pommeroy.]

A few years ago I stayed with my family in a rented house on Martha's Vineyard until the second week in October. The Indian Summer was brilliant and still. We went unwillingly when the time came to go. We took the mid-morning boat to Wood's Hole and drove from a brilliant day at the sea into humid and overcast weather. South of Hartford it began to rain. We reached the apartment house in the east Fifties where we then lived just before dark. The city in the rain seemed particularly cavernous and noisy and the summer was definitely ended. Early the next morning I went to the room where I work. Before leaving the Vineyard I had begun a story, based on some notes made a year or two earlier in New Hampshire. The story described a family in a summer house who spent their evenings playing backgammon. It probably would have been called "The Backgammon Game." I meant to use the checkers, the board and the forfeits of a game to show that the relationships within a family can be extortionate. I was not sure of the story's conclusion but at the back of my mind was the idea that someone would lose his life over the board. I saw a canoe accident on a mountain lake. Reading the story over that morning I saw that, like some kinds of wine, it had not traveled. It was bad.

I come from a Puritanical family and I had been taught as a child that a moral lies beneath all human conduct and that the moral is always detrimental to man: I count among my relations people who feel that there is some inexpungable nastiness at the heart of life and that love, friendship, Bourbon whisky, lights of all kinds—are merely the crudest deceptions. My aim as a writer has been to record a moderation of these attitudes—an escape from them if this seemed necessary—and in the backgammon story I had plainly failed. It was in essence precisely the kind of idle pessimism that I had hoped to enlighten. It was in the vein of one of my elderly uncles who never put a worm on a fish hook without stating that sooner or later we will all be corruption.

In order to occupy myself more cheerfully I looked over the notes I had made during the summer. I first came on a long description of train—sheds and ferry-boat landings—a song to the engines of love and death—but the substance of this was that these journeys were of no import—they were a kind of deception. A few pages after this I came on the description of a friend who, having lost the charms of youth and unable to find any new lights to go by, had begun to dwell on his football triumphs. This was connected to a scathing description of the house in the Vineyard where we had spent a pleasant summer. The house had not been old, but it had been sheathed with old shingles and the new wood of the doors had been scored and stained. The rooms were lighted with electric candles and I linked this crude sense of the past to my friend's failure to mature. The failure, my notes said, was national. We had failed to mature as a people and had turned back to dwell on old football triumphs, raftered ceilings, candlelight and open fires. There were some tearful notes on the sea, washing away the embers of our picnic fires, on the east wind—the dark wind—on the promiscuity of a beautiful young woman I know, on the hardships of island farming, on the jet planes that bombed an island off Gay Head, and a morose description of a walk on South Beach. The only cheerful notes in all this were two sentences about the pleasure I had taken one afternoon in watching my wife and another young lady walk out of the sea without any clothes on.

It is brief, but most journeys leave us at least an illusion of improved perspective and there was a distance that morning between myself and my notes. I had spent the summer in excellent company and in a landscape that I love, but there was no hint of this in the journal I had kept. The conflict in my feelings and my indignation at this division formed quickly in my mind the image of a despicable brother and I wrote: "Goodbye,

My Brother." The story moved quickly. Lawrence arrived on the island on a voyage of no import. I made the narrator fatuous since there was some ambiguity in my indignation. Laud's Head had the accommodating power of an imaginary landscape where you can pick and choose from a wide range of memory, putting in the smell of roses from a very different place and the ringing of a tennis-court roller that you heard years ago. The plan of the house was clear to me at once, although it was unlike any house that I had even seen. The terrace, the living-room, the staircase all appeared in order and when I pushed open the door from the pantry into the kitchen I seemed to find there a cook who had worked for my mother-in-law the year before the year before last. I had brought Lawrence home and taken him through his first night at Land's Head before it was time for me to walk home for supper.

In the morning I unloaded onto Lawrence's shoulders my observations about backgammon. The story was moving then towards the boat club dance. Ten years ago at a costume ball in Minneapolis a man had worn a football uniform and his wife a wedding dress and this recollection fitted easily into place. The story was finished by Friday and I was happy for I know almost no pleasure greater than having a piece of fiction draw together incidents as disparate as a dance in Minneapolis and a backgammon game in the mountains so that they relate to one another and confirm that feeling that life itself is creative process, that one thing is put purposefully upon another, that what is lost in one encounter is replenished in the next and that we possess some power to make sense of what takes place.

On Saturday I took a train to Philadelphia with a friend to see a football game. The story was still on my mind but when I thought back over what I had written, looking for weakness or crudeness, I felt assured. The football game was dull. It got cold. I began to feel uneasy at the half. We left in the middle of the fourth quarter. I had not worn a top-coat and I was shivering. Waiting in the cold for the train back to New York I saw the true worthlessness of my story, the scope of my self-deceptions, the flights and crash-landings of an unstable disposition and when the train came into the station I thought vaguely of throwing myself onto the tracks; but I went instead to the club car and drank some whisky. I have read the story since, and while I see that Lawrence lacks dimension and that the ambiguity will estrange some readers, it remains a reasonably exact account of my feelings after returning to Manhattan after a long summer on Martha's Vineyard.

> —John Cheever, "What Happened." *Understanding Fiction*, edited by Cleanth Brooks and Robert Penn Warren. (New York: Appelton-Century-Crofts, 1959): pp. 570–72.

JAMES E. O'HARA ON MORAL COMPLEXITY

[James E. O'Hara is Associate Professor of English at Pennsylvania State University's York Campus, and has published studies on Cheever, John O'Hara, William Shakespeare, and Sir Phillip Sydney. In the following excerpt, he discusses the story's Cain and Abel theme, in which the Abel brother is, in his persistent virtue and his ultimate victimization, the "bad" brother, as well as the role of Anna, the cook.]

A different kind of ambiguity pervades "Goodbye, My Brother" (1951), a story in which Cheever breaks new ground and explores a theme that clearly absorbed a great deal of his psychic energy. Once again the subject matter is inherently difficult, and the moral question it raises is exceptionally complex. But this time the story's resolution of the issues it raises is very decisive. In this retelling of the biblical Cain and Abel conflict, good and evil are not always easy to separate, and the "bad" brother is actually the victim of violence.

The story is set at "Laud's Head ... on the shore of one of the Massachusetts islands" (3), more specifically at a beachfront house owned by the Pommeroy family, its central focus. Its true location, however, is that border area of the New England spirit that Nathaniel Hawthorne so expertly delineated in stories like "The Maypole of Marymount" a century before Cheever attempted his own exploration: the mysterious terrain where

Puritan moralist confronts Anglican free thinker in a conflict of opposed wills.

The narrator is one of four grown Pommeroy children who periodically gather at the home with their widowed mother. Three of these siblings—the narrator, his sister Diana, and brother Chaddy—enjoy each other's company and their mother's; the problem is with Lawrence, or "Tifty." (As he often does, Cheever hints at what is to come by having the narrator recall Lawrence's two other nicknames, "Little Jesus" and "the Croaker.") Lawrence's chief characteristic emerges shortly into the story, when all of the adults assemble for cocktails on the terrace "so that we could see the bluffs and the sea and the islands in the east" (5). Their mother offers Lawrence a Martini, and he gruffly asks for some rum instead. The request annoys Mrs. Pommeroy because she considers rum a poor choice and because there is none available. Building on this seemingly minor point, Cheever proceeds to establish the story's central conflict. (Social drinking—often to excess—becomes a pervasive feature in Cheever's fiction starting in the early fifties and continuing until his hospitalization for alcoholism in 1976. In some stories, but surprisingly few, he seems to connect excessive drinking and the psychological problems of his characters.)

Lawrence's disagreeableness, seemingly trivial at first, actually points to a deeper flaw in his character: he invariably tends to search out and fix on the most unpleasant or disturbing aspect of any situation, social or otherwise. When Diana is escorted from the house by an admirer she has met in France, Lawrence stuns the rest of the family by asking, "Is that the one she's sleeping with now?" (6). (...)

To overcome their animus toward Lawrence, the other Pommeroys spend a great deal of time swimming, often (but not always) an activity suggestive of purification in Cheever's fiction. But no matter what the activity or occasion, Lawrence discovers something to disapprove of, some way to make those around him miserable. Even Mrs. Pommeroy's cook Anna suffers under the glare of his uprightness. Tifty's interference in her affairs takes the form of a patronizing concern that succeeds only in alienating her, as she explains to the narrator: "He is so skinny but he is always coming into my kitchen to pity me, but I am as good as him, I am as good as *anybody*—" (11).

Like many of Cheever's fictional servants, Anna never rises above the level of caricature, yet her function here is important: she establishes the fact that like the communist Girsdansky of "In Passing," Lawrence is a stern idealist with no real constituency, a preacher without a following. If it is true that most of us are reasonably content with our lives most of the time, someone with as dour a view of life as Lawrence stands little chance of redeeming us.

The message of "Goodbye, My Brother" has further ramifications, however. Anna is content and even happy with her "menial" life (actually she loves to cook and is as obsessed with the need to feed people as Lawrence is driven to unsettle them), and on another level so is the narrator satisfied with his (he is happily married and teaches at a private secondary school). But the attention Cheever lavishes on the raw beauty of the New England seacoast and the vacationers at play on it offers a better insight into the story's ultimate meaning: "We drove back to Laud's Head. It had been a brilliant afternoon, but on the way home we could smell the east wind—the dark wind, as Lawrence would have said—coming in from the sea" (14–15). Above and beyond the preoccupations of everyday life, such passages suggest, there are moments or days when the heavens open to reveal the truth that life can be fine and beautiful, if only we allow it to be. Lawrence is not prepared to admit this, and that is why his brother, with some deliberation, almost kills him.

—James E. O'Hara, "The Short Fiction: A Critical Analysis." *John Cheever: A Study of the Short Fiction* (Boston: Twayne, 1988): pp. 29–30, 31–32.

PATRICK MEANOR ON BIBLICAL AND PURITAN REFERENCES

[Patrick Meanor is the author of *Bruce Chatwin* in the Twayne English Author series, and the editor of *American Short-Story Writers since World War II*. Here, he points out how "Goodbye, My Brother" is Cheever's first triumph with a complicated longer narrative, a narrative as rich as a novel in its use of moral, geographical, and historical allusions, and finds this Cheever's most successful depiction of the brother to brother conflict.]

A close analysis of "Goodbye, My Brother" reveals that Cheever had mastered longer and more complex narrative structures, structures that allowed him to include history (both genealogical and national), geography, myth, and religion, as well as a more sophisticated use of proper names (persons and places), as active agents involved in developing the story. All of these narrative components take on more than their surface appearance and substantially expand a story of family conflict into mythic dimensions. "Goodbye, My Brother" is a much deeper exploration of the love/hate dilemma than is Cheever's "The Brothers." It shows that Cheever had developed into a significantly more sophisticated writer.

"Goodbye, My Brother" is so richly textured that it could serve as Cheever's earliest model of a story that can be discussed and analyzed in terms of recurring mythic patterns, historical allusions and parallels, geographical significance, and brilliant fluctuations of light and dark that eventually evolve into a Manichean battleground. His use of proper names of characters and places enriches the interpretative possibilities and adds a quiet but distinct comic subtext to an already vivid array of characters and plot twists.

Cheever encourages biblical resonances of the Cain/Abel myth when it is obvious that "Goodbye, My Brother" is about an attempted fratricide—the unnamed narrator literally tries to inflict great harm, if not death, on his impossibly Puritanical brother, Lawrence, at the story's dramatic conclusion. But it is crucial that the reader understand that the story is also about the life-denying Puritanical nay-sayers versus the life-affirming yea-sayers. The narrator states that Lawrence reminds him of a Puritan cleric (*SJC*, 6), alluding to a family connection with Cotton Mather himself, America's earliest and most dour Calvinist. Even more important, the summer house, or Eden, of the Pommeroy family is called Laud's Head, a name which, if one knows some English religious history, undoubtedly refers to one of the most famous Anglican Archbishops, William Laud, who was beheaded by the Puritans in 1645 for attempting to bring back into the Episcopal Church music, ritual, the Communion table, and the sacramental system the Puritans had banned. The humorous pun on "Head" and its reappearance on the other side of the Atlantic involved in the same basic conflict demonstrates not only the depth of Cheever's knowledge of English history but his wry sense of humor. And Lawrence is also "all head" and no heart—litigious and icy and a bore. The family name, Pommeroy, means in French "king of the apples"—apples being the single most important metaphor in Cheever's entire literary vocabulary because they evoke an Edenic innocence and childlike happiness that these Pommeroys are trying to regenerate during their summer vacation. One of Cheever's earliest stories is the first of what will become *The World of Apples* in 1973, his sixth short-story collection.

Lawrence Pommeroy is consistently associated with the dark, the sinister, and the east. Cheever is using the east not in its usual association as the source of light and life, the sun, however, but in connection with the encroachment of the Puritanical darkness of the bleak, dogmatic severity of Lawrence's and, by extension, the Puritans' joyless lives. Lawrence is, after all, a lawyer, and his name symbolizes his fractious rigidity. The narrator calls him a "dark figure" as he leaves the family at the story's conclusion. Earlier in the story, the narrator describes Lawrence's effect on the family's attempts to enjoy themselves: "He looked at us all bleakly. The wind and the sea had risen, and I thought that if he heard the waves, he must hear them only as a dark answer to all his dark questions" (*SJC*, 13). Lawrence is also associated with "the east wind—the dark wind, as Lawrence would have said" (*SJC*, 15). The narrator suggests a kind of mystical collusion when he states that "the easterly fog seemed to play into my misanthropic brother's hands" (*SJC*, 16).

Chaddy Pommeroy, the third brother, and Chucky Ewing, the organizer of the country-club dance and the party games, which Lawrence refuses to participate in, both have names that are cognates of Charles and, of course, Archbishop Laud supported and was supported by Charles I, who also lost his head to the Puritans under the chief Roundhead, Oliver Cromwell, because the king had tried to oust the Puritans from political power. Lawrence is also against drinking, accuses his mother of being an alcoholic, refuses to play cards, abhors dancing, and eschews all activities that Puritans considered sinful. Most important, however, he considers all of these activities "a waste of time," the major reason Lawrence gives for prematurely leaving the family after his brother tries to "crown" him. And since the Puritans were obsessed with time and apocalypse, their vision of the world was essentially eschatological, which is why Lawrence's life has become a litany of gloomy good-byes. Indeed, toward the end of the story, Lawrence reveals to his family that his primary purpose in returning to their summer home was to say goodbye; he wants to sell his equity in the house to Chaddy. (Mother Pommeroy's winter home is Philadelphia, an ironic detail since it is the City of Brotherly Love, and this story is about the opposite.) Cheever brilliantly lists the thirteen "goodbyes" that have traced the map of Lawrence Pommeroy's life, one of which, in keeping with the seventeenth-century Puritan conflicts, is his "saying goodbye to the Protestant Episcopal Church" (*SJC*, 18).

Cheever counterbalances the dark, Calvinist gloom of Lawrence and his biblically subservient wife Ruth and their two sad and fearful children with the sensually alluring Helen, Diana, and Odette (an allusion to Proust's seductive Odette de Crécy from *Swann's Way*). The mythic resonances of the goddess of the hunt, Diana, Helen of Troy, and the "promiscuous" Odette are impossible to ignore. This fecund trinity of Dionysians and their celebration of the physical body are Cheever's response to the dark denial and shame of the Puritan ethos that his story clearly condemns. Lawrence is deeply agitated when he hears his mother, on three occasions, invite the family into the "fabulous" pleasures of summer. And he is infuriated when he hears the narrator repeat three times: "It's only a summer day." Cheever articulated as clearly as he ever did his stance as a late American romantic, firmly grounded in the tradition of Ralph Waldo Emerson, Henry David Thoreau, and especially Walt Whitman in "Goodbye, My Brother." In a scene in which he welcomes the transforming powers of the activity of swimming as members of his family unconsciously try to shed some of "Lawrence's rebukes," he celebrates the "mythology of the Atlantic" and "the curative powers of the sea" (*SJC*, 16). And later in the story, in contemplating the grim life of Ruth, Lawrence's wife, he juxtaposes the mystically regenerative power of nature with Ruth's "expiatory passion" and "penitential fervor" (*SJC*, 19).

Once Lawrence and his sad family are gone, the landscape lights up and their Eden is vividly regenerated: "I got up and went to the window and what a morning that was! The wind was northerly. The air was clear. In the early heat, the roses in the garden smelled like strawberry jam." He bestows the light with a quasi-sacramental aura, calling it "the grace of the light" that unifies the sea with the sun, an image that has become one of Cheever's most profoundly visionary epiphanies, but not before detailing Lawrence's crimes against nature: "Oh, what can you do with a man like that? What ran you do? ... How can you teach him to respond to the inestimable greatness of the race, the harsh surface beauties of life? ... The sea that morning was iridescent and dark. My wife and my sister were swimming—and I saw their uncovered heads, black and gold in the dark water. I saw them come out and I saw that they were naked, unshy, beautiful, and full of grace, and I watched the naked women walk out of the sea" (*SJC*, 21). In essence, Cheever has recreated the primordial birth of life and the imagination in nature by reconstituting these modern goddesses in their preternatural innocence. He extends the concept of grace beyond a limited Christian application to include the world of classical mythology that was always grounded in natural cycles.

—Patrick Meanor, "A Writing Machine." *John Cheever Revisited* (New York: Random House, 1988): pp. 43–46

SCOTT DONALDSON ON THE AUTHOR'S ATTITUDE TOWARDS BROTHERHOOD

[Scott Donaldson began his career as a newspaper reporter but is now best known for his biographies of

Hemingway, Fitzgerald, and Cheever. In the following excerpt he discusses "Goodbye, My Brother" in relation to Cheever's feelings towards his real-life brother Fred.]

"Goodbye, My Brother" obviously represents an attempt at exorcising the dark brother. What is less clear is that the brother lies both within and without, just as Cheever had a brother he simultaneously loved and hated and was himself inhabited by both the demon of depression and the angel of joy. The clue is that Tifty does and says very little to deserve the narrator's judgment that he's a "gloomy son of a bitch." Almost all of his "sad frame of mind" is attributed to him by the supposedly cheerful narrator. But it is easy to miss this point, as most readers have done. In first draft, "Goodbye, My Brother" was not the story of two brothers at all. There was only the narrator; Lawrence did not exist. And even in the final version the narrator supplies most of Lawrence's opinions. In a widely quoted passage at the end of the story the narrator asks, "Oh, what can you do with a man like that? What can you do? How can you dissuade his eye in a crowd from seeking out the cheek with acne, the infirm hand; how can you teach him to respond to the inestimable greatness of the race, the harsh surface beauty of life; how can you put his finger for him on the obdurate truths before which fear and horror are powerless?" These questions are directed not at any second party, but at a portion of himself—and the narrator, almost surely, spoke for the author.

The close and curious relationship between Cheever and his real brother was complicated when, in 1952, Fred and Iris Cheever and their four children moved to Briarcliff Manor, the town adjoining Scarborough, and the brothers became neighbors. As advertising manager of the Pepperell Manufacturing Company, Fred had been working out of New York and weekending at his home in the Boston suburbs for several years. When he decided to move the family to Westchester, it was natural that he should have found a place near that of his younger brother. John was not pleased, however. He and Mary dutifully entertained Fred and Iris, but John did not want them as intimate members of their social circle. The brothers' wives did not get along at all. Besides, by the 1950s Fred had started the descent to the depths of alcoholism John would later undergo. On one occasion, John arranged a mixed-doubles badminton game at a local gym involving Eddie Newhouse, an accomplished club player, and Fred Cheever, who played only a backyard game. Newhouse and his partner won easily, and then Eddie swatted the bird back and forth with Fred. "Quit clowning around," yelled John from the sidelines. "Why don't you two play a set?" But eight or ten people were watching, Newhouse knew he would have trouble losing a point—much less a game—to Fred Cheever, and he would have none of it. John seemed to want his brother badly beaten, Newhouse thought.

The fratricidal impulse inherent in the bloodied head, the slaughter by shuttlecock, and—as imagined—the near-fatal shove out the window crops up repeatedly in Cheever's fiction. Sometimes the dark brother is a real character, given a name, rivalrous over a girl or a piece of furniture. Sometimes he is an alter ego determined to obliterate all that is valuable and worthy in oneself. In either case the drive to destroy this other is strong, even though it is accompanied almost always by a corresponding compulsion to care for and nurture him. After the narrator in "Goodbye, My Brother" finally lashes out at his brother Tifty, he is beset by contradictory inclinations. He wants to do away with his saturnine brother, but he also wants to play the Samaritan and bind up his wounds—and that is what he does.

Such contradictory impulses warred within John Cheever as well. "Did you ever want to kill Fred?" his daughter asked him in a 1977 interview. "Well," Cheever replied, "once I was planning to take him trout fishing up at Cranberry Lake, which is just miles away from everything in the wilderness, and I realized if I got him up there he would fall overboard, I would beat him with an oar until he stayed. Of course," he added, "I was appalled by this."

—Scott Donaldson, "Career/1951–1956." *John Cheever: A Biography* (New York: Random House, 1988): pp. 139–141

"The Enormous Radio"

With "The Enormous Radio" (1947), one of the earliest efforts collected in *Stories*, Cheever moved beyond his former reputation of a raconteur of manners and established his new role as a mythologist of the everyday. "The Enormous Radio" is Cheever at his purest, his wildest, and also his most simple. Like most fables, it serves as its own interpretation, and finishes with a fable's cleanness. Indeed, the words that Cheever uses to describe its principal character, Jim Westcott, could be applied to the story itself—"earnest, vehement, and intentionally naïve."

"The Enormous Radio" is not a happy story, though it is an immensely funny one. Jim and Irene Westcott are average, indeed, surreally so. Their situation is one that is "reached by the statistical reports in college alumni bulletins." They have two children, are married for just under a decade, live in a pretty, although not opulent neighborhood, and they go to the theatre, as Cheever anthropologically observes, "on an average of 10.3 times a year." Irene Westcott has a "fine, wide forehead upon which nothing at all ha[s] been written." In these first few paragraphs, Cheever the storyteller adopts the role of a scientist prepping for a ghastly experiment. Since his subjects are so impossibly mediocre, one is quite eager to see the dreadful results.

The only thing that distinguishes the Westcotts from their equally ordinary acquaintances is an inordinate fondness for classical music—not a habit that could be called perverse, certainly, but heterodox enough that it will be the source of their downfall. One day the old radio breaks and Jim orders a new one, a gargantuan, hideous machine. But this new radio, despite its modern fixings, does not play music. Rather, it plays the dramas occuring in the building's other apartments, a realization that gradually dawns upon Jim and Irene as they recognize the cocktail party from Apartment 11-B and the British nurse in Apartment 17-E. At first, the Westcotts find this amusing—in fact, their first evening with their new toy leaves them "weak with laughter." But early the next morning, Irene hears a conversation between an aging couple—one of whom is gravely ill—and is disquieted.

During the course of the entire next day she listens, and when she goes out, she contemplates other people's secrets. Suddenly, her pretty Sutton Place building is infected with whores, misers, and abusers. The lovely morning sunlight is invaded with "demonstrations of indigestion, carnal love, abysmal vanity, faith, and despair." The apparent gaiety of cocktail parties is undermined when Irene hears a couple discussing a diamond left by one of their guests ("…we could use a couple of hundred bucks") and another hostess instructing her maid, "Don't give the best Scotch to anyone who hasn't white hair." The next night, after another day by the radio, Irene is in tears. Their neighbors have been fighting since the morning, and the husband is now beating the wife. "Life is too terrible, too sordid, and awful," Irene weeps. Jim fixes the radio, and it seems as though everything has returned to normal, except that when he comes home that night, the Westcotts quarrel with a fury to rival any of the fights that the radio has ever broadcast.

Cheever's hypothesis, of course, is that discord is not innate to our natures—rather, it is caused by an awareness that it exists. It is a theme that is common in Cheever—the Westcotts fall from grace, with the radio functioning as Pandora's Box or, if you will, Eden's apple, and whatever other temptations of knowledge that have stumbled mankind. The Westcotts are neither virtuous nor particularly honest; still, before the radio, they are blameless because they are unaware that they have ever committed anything blameworthy. "We've always been good and decent and loving to one another, haven't we?" Irene insists, but it becomes clear that discord, once it takes hold, clings like a disease. The next night, Jim provides a ruthless catalogue of his wife's past:

> "You stole your mother's jewelry before they probated her will. You never gave your sister a cent of that money that was intended for her—not even when she needed it. You made Grace Howland's life miserable, and where was all your piety and your virtue when you went to that abortionist?"

It is clear that he has never condemned her in this way, because, technically, before the existence of the radio, Irene has never committed wrong. It is only now that the Westcotts are aware of wrong that their past actions curdle into actual sin. Pre-radio, the Westcotts inhabited a kind of Eden, granted, a dull sounding complacency encapsulated by "college bulletin statistics," but for them it is a paradise all the same. It is fitting that Irene, in her moment of despair, should find herself longing to hear the sound of the British nurse who chants nursery rhymes a few apartments away. The Wescotts are children, after all, and their contact with the radio is their coming-of-age. It is also appropriate that Irene should be the one who discovers the radio's temptation and succumbs to its charms, waking early on the sly to listen and staying next to it during the day, because her precursors in the Western tradition, Eve and Pandora, were also female.

The radio, of course, is the major player in the story, having more personality than both of the irritatingly tame Westcotts combined. It floods with "malevolent green light" and looms over the living room like an "aggressive intruder." But it is its "mistaken sensitivity to discord," that endows it with a beautiful life. If the radio is Pandora's box and Eden's apple, it is also every gossip-monger that we have ever known, the person whose ears are pressed against every wall to hear the sour note in every exchange. Like Lawrence Pommeroy of "Goodbye, My Brother," the radio seeks the "acned cheek." But the radio is more powerful than Lawrence. You cannot question a radio because a radio does not judge, it merely transmits.

The marvel, though, is the deftness with which Cheever chooses to tell this grim parable. "The Enormous Radio" is enormously effective as a cautionary tale, but what really wins us is its style. The outrageously scientific spirit with which Cheever begins the story also finishes it, as the person who gets the last word is the evening newscaster, and his facts are delicious, "A fire in a Catholic hospital near Buffalo for the care of blind children was extinguished early this morning by nuns. The temperature is forty-seven." There is a wonderfully calculated quality to the story. "You love me don't you?" Irene asks her husband, "And we're not hypercritical or worried about money or dishonest, are we?" In his tightwad, middle class, mundane tirade, Jim will answer her for all of her concerns—by accusing her of not paying her clothing bills and then lying about it. This is not heavy-handed moralizing. Instead, it is a moral tale that blends everyday complacence with an astute, darkly comic glimpse into the human condition. We have to laugh, and not at the expense of the Westcotts. Rather, we laugh at our own hapless realization that in reading "The Enormous Radio," we also glimpse our own capacity for spite.

"The Enormous Radio"

Jim Westcott is an average man in his thirties with an earnest and youthful disposition, a wife he loves, two young children, and an apartment at Sutton Place. He is also competent. When the radio that he and his wife enjoy listening to breaks, he buys a new one to replace it. When the new radio broadcasts the goings-on in their apartment building, he calls someone in to fix it. But at the end of the story, Jim Westcott finds himself driven to an uncharacteristic tirade in which he accuses his wife of being unnatural and monstrous—a woman who lies, spends carelessly, steals her mother's jewelry, swindles her own sister, and gets an abortion without the slightest modicum of regret.

Irene Westcott is a woman of modest looks with "a wide, fine forehead upon which nothing at all had been written." Like her husband at the beginning of the story, she is innocent, complacent in her satisfying life. It is Irene, however, who first discovers the flaw in the new radio, and eventually, it is she who finds herself drawn to its broadcasts. At first she finds it amusing, but then it begins to trouble her. As the dramas in the neighboring apartments escalate, so does her horror and her addictive listening. She plays the allegorical female role of Eve or Pandora who falls for the temptation of knowledge, bringing her husband down with her.

CRITICAL VIEWS ON
"The Enormous Radio"

BURTON KENDLE ON THE AUTHOR'S
REINTERPRETATION OF EDEN

[Burton Kendle is Professor Emeritus of English at
Roosevelt University and has written on Ross Macdonald.
Here, he argues that Cheever's reinterpretation of the
creation story in "The Enormous Radio" is a fall, not from
innocence to evil, but from assumed innocence to self-
consciousness.]

Though much less overt in its use of mythology than his recent
"Metamorphoses," and "Mene, Mene, Tekel, Upharsin," John
Cheever's "The Enormous Radio" derives much of its power
from an ironic reinterpretation of the Eden story that helps to
universalize what might otherwise appear to be merely a brilliant
study of mid-century urban discontent. The chief characters, Jim
and Irene Westcott, are appropriately typical representatives of
their class and "seem to strike that satisfactory average of
income, endeavor, and respectability that is reached by the
reports in college alumni bulletins." Their life is comfortably
commonplace, except for their sensitivity to classical music that
both precipitates and explains their response to the radio. Eve's
hubris seems ironically paralleled by Irene's somewhat self-
consciously developed sensitivity. Significantly, the purchase of
the radio is attributed to Jim's uxoriousness; he wants not only to
keep his promise, but also to produce "a surprise for her...."

Cheever develops the motif of innocence by details like Irene's
"wide, fine forehead upon which nothing at all had been
written," and Jim's youthfulness: "he dressed in the clothes his
class had worn at Andover, and his manner was earnest,
vehement, and intentionally naive." The radio, an appropriately
ugly instrument that looks "like an aggressive intruder" to Irene,
is the Satanic invader of the Westcotts' world of apparent
innocence. Like her archetypal parallel, Irene is the first to

become aware of the radio's "mistaken sensitivity to discord," though not of the significance of this discord. Eve's momentary illusion of godhead, and Irene's brief elation over the possibilities of supposed omniscience are similarly undercut by later occurrences in their lives.

Initially, Jim seems less disturbed by the knowledge revealed through the radio than by the effect of this knowledge on his wife, but gradually the combined forces of the radio and Irene's growing anxiety cause him to articulate an insight into the nature of evil more searching than any Irene can experience. Even before the radio starts broadcasting conversations from neighboring apartments, its mere presence in the household oppresses the atmosphere: "Jim was too tired to make even a pretense of sociability, and there was nothing about the dinner to hold Irene's interest, so her attention wandered from the food, to the deposits of silver polish on the candlesticks...."

Once the radio does begin to tune in to the lives of the Westcotts' neighbors, the conversations of an elderly couple, overheard at night, make clear to Irene the sinister implications of the knowledge she is acquiring: "The unrestrained [*sic*: restrained] melancholy of the dialogue and the draft from the bedroom window made her shiver, and she went back to bed." The next morning, further conversations transmitted by the radio "astonished and troubled her," and this increasing disillusion about the hidden lives of her neighbors carries over to a luncheon, where she "looked searchingly at her friend and wondered what her secrets were."

Irene's interest in the Salvation Army band during the couple's walk to a dinner party, like her obsession with the Sweeney's nurse, is a desperate, if shallow attempt to maintain a belief in the reality of human goodness, ultimately her own. Predictably, the attempt fails: at the dinner, Irene "interrupted her hostess rudely and stared at the people across the table from her with an intensity for which she would have punished her children." A self-righteous aversion to the possible covert evil of others, and an intensifying conviction of her own virtue impede any meaningful learning experience for her.

The final scene of the story, carefully foreshadowed by the

growing tensions in the household, reveals the unstable basis of the Westcotts' edenic world. Jim's anxieties indicate that the initial portrait of him was ironically misleading: "I'm not getting any younger, you know. I'm thirty-seven. My hair will be grey next year. I haven't done as well as I'd hoped to do. And I don't suppose things will get any better." The phrase "intentionally naive," used in the introductory description of Jim, had unobtrusively exposed his air of innocence as a rather desperate pose. In a passage reinforcing mythic parallels, Jim stresses Irene's guilt as the major cause of his grief and ridicules her assumptions of personal virtue: "Why are you so Christly all of a sudden? What's turned you overnight into a convent girl? You stole your mother's jewelry before they probated her will. You never gave your sister a cent of that money that was intended for her—not even when she needed it. You made Grace Howland's life miserable, and where was all your piety and your virtue when you went to that abortionist? I'll never to forget how cool you were. You packed your bag and went off to have that child murdered as if you were going to Nassau."

Irene's final futile attempt to tune in the Sweeneys' nurse, the positive image of humanity needed to reinforce a belief in her own goodness, illuminates the terrors of assumed omniscience and the inevitable defeat of human pride. The detached voice of the announcer, mingling disasters with weather reports, is a twentieth-century version of a divine edict that permanently exiles the Westcotts, but offers no parallel to the ultimate promise traditionally associated with the original pair. The ironic reinterpretation given the myth by Cheever suggests that the expulsion from Eden does not symbolize the fall from good to evil, or from innocence to experience, but the fall from assumed innocence to awareness, specifically self-awareness, and its attendant anguish. Cheever's irony implies that man's knowledge of his personal evil, no matter how painfully acquired, does not bring the power conventionally attributed to such insight, but only additional difficulties and frustrations. Both Adam and Jim are exiled to a life of constant anxiety and fruitless bickering.

—Burton Kendle, "Cheever's Use of Mythology in 'The Enormous Radio,'" *Studies in Short Fiction* 4 (Spring 1967): 262–64.

Henrietta Ten Harmsel on Parallels to Nathaniel Hawthorne's "Young Goodman Brown"

[Henrietta Ten Harmsel is Professor Emerita of English at Calvin College, and is translator of an anthology of Dutch Christian Poetry, *So Much Sky*. In the following, she argues against Burton Kendle's Edenic reading of "The Enormous Radio" and compares Cheever's story to Hawthorne's "Young Goodman Brown," with the radio assuming the role of the devil.]

Burton Kendle's analysis of Cheever's "The Enormous Radio" (*Studies in Short Fiction*, 4 [1967], 262–264) perceptively clarifies the change from apparent innocence to disturbing self-knowledge in Jim and Irene Westcott. Comparing the malevolent radio to a powerful Satanic intruder is also very sound. However, associating "The Enormous Radio" with the Eden story seems to me less enlightening than comparing it with Hawthorne's "Young Goodman Brown." In both of these stories the "innocent" protagonists are made aware of an evil that already quite definitely exists, in themselves as well as their societies. In both it is partly the deceptive façades of their societies—certainly not Edenic—that have made honest acknowledgement of evil impossible. And in both, the leading protagonist is left finally in this deep dilemma: the necessity and yet the apparent impossibility of maintaining love when the corruption of both the individual and his society has been overwhelmingly exposed.

In the two stories the development from innocence to self-knowledge is amazingly similar. Initially Irene's pleasantly blank forehead and Jim's intentional naiveté resemble the pretty "pink-ribboned" head of Faith and Goodman Brown's dubious affirmation of his innocent intentions. The mysterious, black-clad figure whom the uneasy Goodman meets in the forest is hard for him to recognize in spite of the devil's snake-like staff. So also Irene becomes immediately uneasy at the malevolence of the "aggressive intruder" but fails to comprehend its power as she turns the "dials and switches ... disappointed and bewildered." As the radio progresses from violently amplified music to crackling static to electric razors, Irene meets each new development with the decision to "turn It off." In a similar manner Goodman Brown punctuates each deeper move into the evil forest with his determination to "go no farther." The radio's "mistaken sensitivity to discord" is like the devil's recounting of only the evils in Goodman's society: the lashing of Quaker women and the secret burial of illegitimate infants. These revelations of unrecognized evils parallel the obscenity, the dishonesty, and the lechery that the radio reveals to Irene in her neighbors. As young Goodman Brown slowly recognizes Goody Cloyse, Deacon Gookin, and the "confused and doubtful ... voices" from the "depths of the cloud" above him, so Irene begins to identify the voices of Miss Armstrong, the Fullers, and the Osborns in 16-C.

Just as the "horrible laughter" of Goodman Brown changes later to the sadness of "a darkly meditative, a distrustful, if not a desperate man," so Irene's laughter changes later to furtive guilt and hysterical tears. Goodman Brown's self-righteous hesitations and his final desperate advice to Faith to "resist the wicked one" are also somewhat reflected in Irene's actions: her sad attempt to do "a good deed in a naughty world," her desperate plea to Jim to intervene in the Osborn's struggles, and her painful insistence that she and Jim "have never been like that." Indeed Hawthorne's forest music that "seemed a hymn" but proved to be the "awful harmony" of individual and social corruption is not unlike the soothing classical music that the enormous radio changes to the thin scratchy music of "The Missouri Waltz" and the horrible cacophony of life in the surrounding apartments. Finally, in both stories the malevolent intruder is suddenly removed: the radio is fixed and the devil of Goodman Brown's "vision" disappears. But things are no longer the same. Young Goodman Brown now sees only evil in those whom he formerly loved, even in Faith, into whose face he looks "sternly and sadly." All harmony has also disappeared for Jim and Irene: he reveals his financial insecurity, resentfully shouts "turn it off" to Irene's guilty fears, and finally enumerates cruelly all the secret sins of her past. But, like the

Goodman, Irene can no longer suppress her vision of her pervasive guilt. "Disgraced and sickened" she stands, unable to turn the radio off.

Although both stories do somewhat resemble the Eden tale, they both reveal also a basic difference from it: that a perverted society is partially responsible for the individual's unrealistic "innocence" and isolation. Hawthorne is obviously exposing the hypocritical purity of a community that refuses to acknowledge its sin, making honest human relationships impossible. Cheever is obviously criticizing a society in which technology and compartmentalized urban living are making human understanding and communication impossible. The old radio at the beginning of the story is still "sensitive, unpredictable," and responsive to a human strike of the hand. But when it is "beyond repair," it is replaced by the enormous, ugly radio whose confounding "number of dials and switches" makes it a fitting symbol of the burgeoning forces of uncontrollable technology. In such a society "scratchy music" and the superficial "Whiffenpoof Song" replace the classics. The real significance of human relationships seems to be "lost forever" like the Schubert melody. Instead, Jim's purchasing of a more intricately technological machine is supposed to bring satisfaction: "I bought this damned radio to give you some pleasure.... I paid a great deal of money for it. I thought it might make you happy." Although the repaired radio finally does broadcast Schiller's "Ode to Joy," it is obvious from their bickering that Jim and Irene have paid too high a price for technological advancement. Even more than hypocritical Puritanism, growing technology engenders devils which dehumanize men.

Like Hawthorne's story, Cheever's also proceeds and concludes in ambiguities. One hardly knows whether the radio—like Hawthorne's devil—represents a surrealistic nightmare or "the real thing." Does the radio's final noncommittal announcement of catastrophe—but also of charity "by nuns"—suggest that some remnant of "Faith" may live on to accompany Irene Westcott to her grave? Like Goodman Brown she may remain "distrustful" and even "desperate." But like him she has learned something significant: the reality of evil cannot be hypocritically or technologically "turned off." Like Hawthorne, Cheever deals basically with the universal dilemma of maintaining a balanced humanity in a world where evil seems to overwhelm the good.

—Henrietta Ten Harmsel, "'Young Goodman Brown' and 'The Enormous Radio,'" *Stuides in Short Fiction* 9 (Fall 1972): 407–8.

JAMES E. O'HARA ON THE CONFLUENCE OF
REALITY AND FABLE

[Here, O'Hara demonstrates how "The Enormous Radio" surpasses the simplicity of its parts, for it is better than both grim moral parable and urban vignette.]

But there is virtually no precedent for the most widely read of Cheever's short stories, a fantastic tale set in a Manhattan apartment. It would be only a slight exaggeration, in fact, to claim that the apartment building in "The Enormous Radio" (1947) is a central character in the story; it is as alive as any of the "real" people in the narrative. The animation of inanimate structures is an ancient literary device, and such writers as Émile Zola had fully explored the thematic possibilities inherent in the technique long before Cheever tried it. Few writers, however, have been able to achieve the intensity of effect that Cheever creates with seeming ease in "The Enormous Radio" by blending realism, fantasy, comedy, and pathos. By carefully manipulating these elements into a structure that is larger than the sum of its parts, Cheever first hypnotizes the reader and then illuminates some of the darker regions of the human psyche.

The story's two main characters, Jim and Irene Westcott, are described in the opening lines as "the kind of people who seem to strike that satisfactory average of income, endeavor, and respectability that is reached by the statistical reports in college alumni bulletins" (33). They are outwardly as normal as can be: productive, law-abiding, the parents of two young children. The teller of the story merely hints at a skeptical view of their life-style (Cheever may even be parodying himself) when he records that the Westcotts go to the theater "on an average of 10.3 times a year" (33).

The only significant difference between the Westcotts and other young couples in their set is their interest in serious music. When their old radio suddenly dies in the middle of a Schubert quartet, Jim decides to buy a replacement. This could serve as the stuff of comedy pure and simple, and in fact Cheever would work on scripts for the *Life with Father* television series only a few years later. A less experienced writer might have succumbed to the comic potential of his narrative premise, but Cheever had other intentions.

The Westcotts soon discover that their new radio can garner sounds and conversations from every corner of their building. At first the narrator suggests that this is due to scene technical oddity in the radio or the building itself, but it quickly becomes apparent that no "logical" explanation will suffice. The radio tunes in quite accurately on the private lives of the building's tenants. The Westcotts eavesdrop on "a monologue on salmon fishing in Canada, a bridge game, running comments on home movies of what had apparently been a fortnight at Sea Island, and a bitter family quarrel about an overdraft at the bank" (37). For awhile this incredible addition to their home strikes the Westcotts as funny, a source of free entertainment beyond their wildest imagining. But the reference to a family quarrel should warn the reader that the story is not simply a comic sketch. The radio takes on tremendous symbolic importance when we realize that the particular form of voyeurism the Westcotts have succumbed to is essentially no different from the "normal" reader's own, supposedly more respectable vice: looking over the narrator's shoulder into the turmoil of his characters' lives. In this light Cheever, or any good storyteller, is our enormous radio, and by extension we are the Westcotts.

Thus "The Enormous Radio" converts a comic premise into a powerfully enlightening narrative engine. In one brilliant stroke, Cheever had both fully exploited and utterly transcended his own cleverness. More than forty years later the idea seems so obvious, and the writing so effortless, that it is easy for us to make the same mistake that some of Cheever's contemporaries made by overlooking the great advance this story represents for its writer and, I think, for the short story as a narrative form. It is an amazingly compact blend of fantasy and stark realism. In the following excerpt, for example, Cheever manages to move Irene from a restaurant back to her apartment, establish the almost magnetic hold of the radio on her consciousness, reinforce the terrible truthfulness of the radio, and advance the theme of pervasive, inescapable duplicity:

> Irene had two Martinis at lunch, and she looked searchingly at her friend and wondered what her secrets were. They had intended to go shopping after lunch, but Irene excused herself and went home. She told the maid she was not to be disturbed; then she went into the living room, closed the doors, and switched on the radio. She heard, in the course of the afternoon, the halting conversation of a woman entertaining her aunt, the hysterical conclusion of a luncheon party, and a hostess briefing her maid about some cocktail guests. "Don't give the best Scotch to anyone who hasn't white hair," the hostess said. "See if you can get rid of that liver paste before you pass those hot things, and could you lend me five dollars? I want to tip the elevator man." (38)

T. S. Eliot has noted that humankind cannot bear too much reality, but Cheever seems determined to give us a strong dose of it; not the least disturbing aspect of "reality" in this case is the obsessive need of the Westcotts to hear it in such a sneaky fashion.

Cheever had achieved economy of style after his first few stories, but he had rarely demonstrated this kind of smooth, assured balance even in his army stories. Having released himself from his addiction to realism, he was clearly enjoying the full exercise of his talent. How many of his readers had at some time or other wanted to spy on their neighbors? Having drawn them in this far, he could now compel them to overhear an eclectic catalog of human folly, by turns humorous and frightening. We finally share in the psychic pain of the Westcotts when, too late, they realize they have heard too much:

"Of course we're happy," he said tiredly. He began to surrender his resentment. "Of course we're happy. I'll have that damned radio fixed or taken away tomorrow." He stroked her soft hair. "My poor girl," he said.

"You love me, don't you?" she asked. "And we're not hypercritical or worried about money or dishonest, are we?"

"No, darling," he said. (40)

But the following day, after the radio has been "fixed" and dutifully tunes in classical music, the Westcotts have a terrible argument—about their own problems with money and dishonesty—as the radio news reports disasters from around the globe. In a masterful demonstration of his storytelling art, Cheever has quietly yanked us out of our fascination with his clever story into an awareness of what we should have known all along: all those Westcotts parading up and down the supermarket aisles of America are every bit as normal and abnormal as we are. The story needs no explicitly stated moral; awareness is the beginning of understanding and sympathy for our fellow humans, and in that direction, Cheever knew, lies salvation.

—James E. O' Hara, "The Short Fiction: A Critical Analysis." *John Cheever: A Study of the Short Fiction* (Boston: Twayne, 1988): pp. 18–21.

PATRICK MEANOR ON THE AUTHOR'S
STYLISTIC BREAKTHROUGH

[In this excerpt, Meanor explains that "The Enormous Radio" is a landmark in Cheever's maturation. He points to the sophisticated use of fantasy, the witty everyday detail, and also asserts that the story is one of Cheever's most fully realized reinterpretations of man's fall from grace.]

It is the first story in which Cheever breaks through his earlier realistic-naturalistic narrative habits to combine elements of realism and fantasy, a combination that expands both the comic and tragic possibilities of his storytelling powers. "The Enormous Radio" is also his earliest and most brilliant version of the "fall" from innocence into experience, from blissful ignorance into the horror of self knowledge, and from a comforting life of illusion into unbearable reality. Cheever has also made setting more than mere location for dramatizing marital conflicts. The apartment building in Manhattan is very much an active agent in the progress of the story. The building, initially their Edenic protection against the evils of the outside world, is transformed into a Dantean Inferno.

Unlike the midwestern pastoral questers or the "fallen" working-class servants and elevator boys in the other stories in this volume, the Westcotts are comfortably swathed in their pastoral dream. Their name comically suggests that they are fully ensconced or housed (as in where one lays one's cot) in the "West"—that is, the location of treasure, the cup of gold, the serenity that awaits them in the Western Isles—the Hebrides and so on. And, content though they seem, they also wish, someday, to move to Westchester. Jim and Irene Westcott's greatest pleasure is listening to classical music on the radio, and when it breaks down in the middle of a Schubert quartet, they must acquire a new one. Jim buys a very large and expensive new radio, and once it's attached, it not only begins to bring in Mozart quintets but also becomes a conduit to the lives in the other apartments in the building. At first, Jim and Irene enjoy the unique position the radio places them in. Privy to many of the private lives in their apartment, they become virtually omniscient—and view themselves as having attained a semi-divine status. At first they revel in their new power, but their arrogance begins to give way to feelings of guilt because they know they are violating the privacy and, therefore, the truth of their neighbors' lives.

The Westcotts' voyeurism not only exposes their neighbors' private vulnerabilities but brings about the major calamity of the story. Concurrent with their discovery of the desperate unhappiness of their neighbors, they fall into catastrophic self-knowledge. Their innocence had consisted in believing that they really lived in an urban Eden. Their fallen condition causes them to doubt everything they had ever believed. Irene discovers that her life is no different from many of her neighbors' lives: "Life is too terrible, too sordid and awful. But we've never been like that, have we darling? ... We are happy, aren't we?" And at the very moment that they see themselves as being just like everyone else, a moment that would comfort "normal" well-adjusted people, their new knowledge totally isolates them, because they see themselves for the first time. Their innocent arrogance had positioned them, they presumed, above the rest of the vulgar crowd, beyond the malady of the quotidian. The fictive scaffolding of their lives now lies fully exposed and, like Adam and Eve, they feel ashamed and turn on each other. Now they must face their financial problems, their entrance into rueful middle age and, most painfully, dreadful memories from their past that they thought they had laid to rest. They cover their vulnerability—their nakedness—by blaming one another for their newly discovered plight. They have discovered the fictiveness of their fictions.

In a sense, "The Enormous Radio" can be considered Cheever's first truly "modern" story, if one uses the term *modern* to refer to narratives no longer concerned primarily with moral dilemmas or issues of right or wrong, good and evil. True modernity, as in one of Cheever's favorite writers, Flaubert, consists of a profound questioning of the very terms of reality and, thus, of how characters "perceive" their experience or, even more disturbing, how they unconsciously "create" realities that protect them from the brutality of time, senseless suffering, and meaningless death. Wallace Stevens defined one of the functions of the imagination as "a violence from within that protects us from a violence without"—that is, without the "violent" power of the imagination within the human psyche serving as a protective shield from brute reality, human consciousness would be overwhelmed and unable to function on a daily basis. Emma Bovary *must* commit suicide once she discovers that life is not a romance novel.

Cheever's craft showed greater narrative and philosophical refinement not only in his ability to create existential quasi-fantasies closer to the "fictions" of Latin-American writers such as Jorge Luis Borges and Julio Cortázar but, just as important, in his willingness to utilize more daring metaphors, such as the radio and the apartment house of the Westcotts. Cheever also uses the metaphor of the "house" as a Jungian symbol of the psyche as the repository of the unconscious. Once the corrupting, serpentine "radio" enters the Westcotts' garden and corrupts their pastoral contentment, they are exposed not only to the heartbreaking contents of their apartment building but, concurrently, to the contents of their "house"—that is, their unconscious psyche unprotected by their "fictions."

—Patrick Meanor, "A Writing Machine." *John Cheever Revisited* (New York: Random House, 1988): pp. 52–54.

"The Five-Forty-Eight"

In "The Five-Forty-Eight" (1954), the protagonist Blake, whom we know only by his surname, is an unfeeling and selfish businessman, a self-righteous sadist, whose "pallor and grey eyes" belie "unpleasant tastes." When his wife forgets to cook supper, he does not speak to her for two weeks, and relishes her daily protests. He does not have a single friend on his daily train ride home although he knows many commuters from his Shady Hill neighborhood. Even ordinary metabolic functions are alien to him; he does not perspire when he is nervous, instead, the rainwater against his neck is a simulation of the sweat that a normal man might exude. Although he appears a gentleman on the surface, garbed as he is in the dark suits that "sumptuary laws" dictate, he has no civility in his heart. Blake is clearly one of Cheever's most sinister creations—a man incapable of emotion, but more dangerous because he has tremendous capacity for cleverness and insight.

Like many Cheever stories, "The Five-Forty-Eight" is not fueled by actual explosive action, but rather by the foreboding that there is something explosive to come. At the opening of the story, Blake emerges from his office only to be followed by a woman, as yet unknown to us. He tries to shake her off, at which point there is a flashback and the woman is properly introduced. Her name, which he has difficulty recalling, is Miss Dent; she worked for a short time as his secretary. She was clearly in awe of her employer, a fact that pleased him, and despite clues about her psychosis—she was recently discharged from a mental hospital— they bedded in her squalid one bedroom apartment. The next day, Blake fired her, and about a month has elapsed since. Hounded by Miss Dent, Blake decides not to catch his original train, but to take refuge in a gentleman's club and to catch the later five-forty-eight express. He sees no sign of her as he eventually boards the train, and then she enters his compartment with a gun hidden in her purse. Blake is surrounded by fellow commuters and neighbors, but sadly enough, he is on friendly terms with none. Miss Dent, therefore, has the acquiescent audience that she desires. First, she forces him to read a letter that she has written for him, in which she addresses him as "beloved," and then she makes him listen to her half-coherent rages about good, evil, and love. When the train stops at Shady Hill, she follows him out of the train and, with the gun pointed at his head, forces him to lie with his face in the dirt. Miss Dent then quits the scene, and Blake is left to make his own way home.

It is not surprising that a man like Blake should seduce his secretary and then dismiss her at lunchtime. Unlike other Cheever characters, he does not do it with any innocence or misgiving. He is interested in his secretary because of the power that he has over her, because she imagines his life as "full of friendships, money, and a large and loving family" and herself has a "peculiar feeling of deprivation." Unfortuately for Blake, Miss Dent is not just lonely and pathetic; as her name might imply, she is insane. Her ghastly handwriting is the key to her broken mind. Blake senses this, for it gives "him the feeling that she had been the victim of some emotional conflict that had in its violence broken the continuity of the lines she was able to make on paper," and he reacts to it with distaste, but is too interested in himself to pay it any more heed.

It is his undoing. When Miss Dent follows him, she trails him with a fury that is only the privilege of the mentally unhinged. She is an exquisite anti-Eurydice as they plunge into the labryinthine structure of New York. "Walking in the city," the narrator explains, "we seldom turn and look back," and Blake never does. Oedipus does not look back because of his love; Blake does not because he simply cannot care. Perhaps it is because he does not look back, however, that he fails to lose his pursuer and she follows him onto the train with a gun in her hand.

Blake's eventual comeuppance is not satisfying. It becomes clear, on the train ride to the suburbs, that Miss Dent wants to eradicate him from the world—not to erase him physically, but to change his soul. Despite the frenzied nature of her accusation, she is quite accurate in her judgment, "...if there are devils in this world, if there are people in this world who represent evil, is it our duty to exterminate them? I know that you always prey on weak people..." He feels nothing and she feels too much. Although at the end he lies prostrate at her feet at gun point, and she says "Now I can wash my hands of you," her mission remains unfulfilled. The only reason why he gets on the floor in the first place is due to his intense interest in self-preservation. There is a wonderful moment that might be interpreted as repentance when Blake, with Miss Dent's gun still aimed at him, hears a distant boat, "a sound that drew slowly behind it across the dark water such a burden of clear, sweet memories of gone summers and gone pleasures that it made his flesh crawl, and he thought of dark in the mountains and children singing." On the verge of death, Blake recalls all the important things of life that he has so heartlessly ignored. But then the gun is taken away, he gets up, and sees that Miss Dent is "small, common, and harmless." Like Lawrence Pommeroy of "Goodbye, My Brother," Blake rises from the ground as the same man.

To author Raymond Carver there is also a lack of closure. He picks up in "The Train" where "The Five-Forty-Eight" leaves off, weaving a tale of existential disconnect as Miss Dent, on her way back to New York, is unable to engage with other passengers waiting for the train who say in response to her feeble attempt at conversation, "Don't know you ... don't want to know you." Slowly she comes to the realization that it is as though the events of the afternoon never occurred, because it does not matter if they have or haven't. As Carver has derived, "The Five-Forty-Eight" is worse than tragic, and it is unsettling because it is so incomplete.

This point is drawn further by Shady Hill's own nothingness. Shady Hill, as its name implies, is a community of mists and fog. Critics liken Shady Hill to the Greek underworld,[1] with its commuter train functioning as the River Styx, and it is appropriate that Blake, as the anti-Oedipus, has led Miss Dent here. It is a world of obscurity, in which no element really connects, where no cycle is fulfilled. Most importantly, it is a world of permanent statis. "What is really wrong," remarks one of Cheever's characters, "...is that it doesn't have a future. So much energy is spent in perpetuating the place ... that the only idea of the future anyone has is just more and more commuting trains and more parties." Tragedy, love, infidelity, and violence do happen in the Shady Hill stories, and yet, the next time we return, it is like they never did.

NOTE

1. Patrick Meanor. *John Cheever Revisited*. Boston: Twayne Publishers, 1995: p. 76.

"The Five-Forty-Eight"

Miss Dent is a quiet woman in her twenties, slender, plain, and dressed in dark clothes. As her name might imply, she is also emotionally imbalanced, and hints of her dementia are sprinkled throughout the narrative—in her frequent references to her being "sick," her stays at a "hospital," and finally, in her angry, scrawling handwriting. She is also a sad and romantic figure, however, someone with a "permanent air of deprivation" who keeps a piano and Beethoven sonatas in her small studio apartment. When her employer seduces her and dismisses her, she follows him onto his commuter train and holds him at gunpoint until she feels like his power play has been reversed.

Blake is a successful business man who commutes into New York City from his home and family in Shady Hill, attired daily in a dark business suit. He is also an unnatural, evil man; his wife fears him and even his colleagues and neighbors stay away. It is indicative that the two people who refuse to talk to him on the train are, successively, his wife's confidante and the father of his son's best friend. When he hires a secretary by the name of Miss Dent, he seduces her because she is so in awe of him, and he fires her the next day. The only emotion, however, that he can feel when Miss Dent confronts him with a pistol, is fear, for Blake is incapable of questioning himself.

"The Five-Forty-Eight"

LYNNE WALDELAND ON THE STORY'S INNAPPROPRIATENESS COMPARED TO THE SHADY HILL STORIES

[Lynne Waldeland is English Professor Emerita and former Provost of Northern Illinois University, and has written about John Cheever and Wright Morris. Here, Waldeland argues that the drama and bitter pessimism of "The Five-Forty-Eight" jar with the positive tone of the other Shady Hill stories.]

"The Five-Forty-Eight," which won the Benjamin Franklin award, differs significantly from the other stories in this collection in that the Shady Hill protagonist is a totally unlikable character with whom we are not intended to sympathize. Cheever's intent here is signaled by his giving the character only a last name, Blake; furthermore, although a wife is mentioned, Cheever gives us no details of children, house, station wagon, or other humanizing data about Blake's life. The story involves an act of vengeance against the man undertaken by a woman he has misused. She was his secretary; he slept with her, then had her fired to avoid complications. Unfortunately for Blake, the woman has a history of mental illness; and after being unable to get in to see him in his office, she follows him to his train, the five-forty-eight to Shady Hill. When he tries to move away, she shows him a gun in her purse. He wishes one of his neighbors on the train would notice his plight, but it is revealed that he has quarreled with the only ones in his car—Mrs. Compton, because she sympathized with Blake's wife after he mistreated her, and Mr. Watkins, for being an artist and free spirit and hence a bad influence in the community—and they understandably ignore him. He is left alone at the station with a madwoman, who apparently wants no more violent revenge than to force him to kneel down in the street and put his face in the dirt. He does so, weeping, and she turns and walks away. The last line of the story, "He got to his feet and picked up his hat from the ground where it had fallen and walked home" (p. 134), in its flat matter-of-factness leaves us believing that no rude awakening into an enlarged humanity has taken place for Blake. The only effect that thinking he is going to die has on him is to make him notice more vividly the homes, the lights, the street signs of Shady Hill, perhaps as symbols of the security which is now in doubt for him; his reflections are marked by no thoughts of family and no regret or guilt about his treatment of the woman. This story is an odd addition to the volume; it adds no real insight into Shady Hill as a community, and it provides the only unrelievedly despicable character from Shady Hill in the book. It is very well paced dramatically, and it achieves its degree of horror by the placement of ominous events in the familiar setting of other stories in the volume. Fictionally, it is a good story, but thematically it is rather out of phase with the rest of the Shady Hill stories.

—Lynne Waldeland, "Love and Usefulness: Life in Shady Hill and Elsewhere." *John Cheever* (Boston: Twayne Publishers, 1979): pp. 70–71.

George W. Hunt on the Relationship between Villainy and Forgetfulness

[George W. Hunt, S.J. is the director of Fordham University's Archbishop Hughes Institute on Religion and Culture. He is the author of *John Updike and the Three Great Secret Things: Sex, Religion, and Art.* In the following exerpt he argues that Blake's central villainy is his lack of self awareness. Hence, because Miss Dent brings memory and awareness back to him, her mission is a success.]

Cheever has compassion for those characters who have little hope but at least are rich in memories. The only rather villainous characters in his fiction are those who are forgetful or without memories of any kind, without self-awareness as pilgrims. Blake, the central character in "The Five-Forty-Eight," is such a man. As the story starts he is oblivious of his past and cannot remember the name of a former mistress who is slightly or totally insane; however, she has not forgotten him—in fact, she is pursuing him with a gun. On the train the girl quotes from Job the lines, "Where shall wisdom be found? Where is the place of understanding? The depth saith it is not in me; the sea saith it is not with me. Destruction and death say we have heard the force with our ears" (*SJC*, p. 243).

The imminence of death and destruction at another's hand— here pointedly taking place on a commuter train, thus joining the routine with the bizarre—makes these *existential* questions for Blake, turning them inward, *reminding* him of other modes of wisdom and understanding. It is significant, then, that this terrifying experience prompts two antipodal memories within him. The first is dire: "He remembered the unburied dead he had seen in the war. The memory came in a rush; entrails, eyes, shattered bone, ordure, and other filth" (p. 245). The second memory is more heartening: "He heard from off the dark river the drone of an outboard motor, a sound that drew slowly behind it across the dark water such a burden of clear, sweet memories of gone summers and gone pleasures that it made his flesh crawl, and he thought of dark in the mountains and the children singing" (pp. 246–247).

These antipodal memories restore Blake briefly to a realization of life's mysteries posed by Job's questions, and yet the story ends with a moving reversal. After the girl humiliates him by forcing his face in the dirt, "he raised himself out of the dust— warily at first, until he saw by her attitude, her looks, that she had forgotten him" (p. 247).

—George W. Hunt, "Themes in Tension." *The Hobgoblin Company of Love* (Grand Rapids, MI: William B. Eardman's Publishing Company, 1983): pp. 88–89.

RAYMOND CARVER'S SEQUEL TO THE STORY

[Raymond Carver was one of twentieth century America's master fiction writers and poets, author of *Where I'm Calling From* and *What We Talk About When*

In the following excerpt, taken from his story "The Train," we follow Miss Dent after she takes her leave from Blake. Because no one is interested in listening to Miss Dent and her adventures, even she begins to forget.]

"You don't say much," the woman said to Miss Dent. "But I'll wager you could say a lot if someone got you started. Couldn't you? But you're a sly boots. You'd rather just sit with your prim little mouth while other people talk their heads off. Am I right? Still waters. Is that your name?" the woman asked. "What *do* they call you?"

"Miss Dent. But I don't know you," Miss Dent said.

"I sure as hell don't know you, either!" the woman said. "Don't know you and don't care to know you. Sit there and think what you want. It won't change anything. But I know what I think, and I think it stinks!"

The old man left his place at the window and went outside. When he came back in a minute later, he had a cigarette burning in his holder and he seemed in better spirits. He carried his shoulders back and his chin out. He sat down beside the woman.

"I found some matches," he said. "There they were, a book of matches right next to the curb. Someone must have dropped them."

"Basically, you're lucky," the woman said. "And that's a plus in your situation. I always knew that about you, even if no one else did. Luck is important." The woman looked over at Miss Dent and said: "Young lady, I'll wager you've had your share of trial and error in this life. I know you have. The expression on your face tells me so. But you aren't going to talk about it. Go ahead then, don't talk. Let us do the talking. But you'll get older. Then you'll have something to talk about. Wait until you're my age. Or his age," the woman said and jerked her thumb at the old man. "God forbid. But it'll all come to you. In its own sweet time, it'll come. You won't have to hunt for it, either. It'll find you."

Miss Dent got up from the bench with her handbag and went over to the water fountain. She drank from the fountain and turned to look at them. The old man had finished smoking. He took what was left of his cigarette from the holder and dropped it under the bench. He tapped the holder against his palm, blew into the mouthpiece, and returned the holder to his shirt pocket. Now he, too, gave his attention to Miss Dent. He fixed his eyes on her and waited along with the woman, Miss Dent gathered herself to speak. She wasn't sure where to begin, but she thought she might start by saying she had a gun in her handbag. She might even tell them she'd nearly killed a man earlier that night.

But at that moment they heard the train. First they heard the whistle, then a clanging sound, an alarm bell, as the guard rails went down at the crossing. The woman and the white-haired old man got up from the bench and moved toward the door. The old man opened the door for his companion, and then he smiled and made a little movement with his fingers for Miss Dent to precede him. She held the handbag against the front of her blouse and followed the older woman outside.

The train tooted its whistle once more as it slowed and then ground to a stop in front of the station. The light on the cab of the engine went back and forth over the track. The two cars that made up this little train were well lighted, so it was easy for the three people on the platform to see that the train was nearly empty. But this didn't surprise them. At this hour, they were surprised to see anyone at all on the train.

The few passengers in the cars looked out through the glass and thought it strange to find these people on the platform, making ready to board a train at this time of night. What business could have taken them out? This was the hour when people should be thinking of going to bed. The kitchens in the houses up on the hills behind the station were clean and orderly; the dishwashers had long ago finished their cycle, all things were in their places. Night-lights burned in children's bedrooms. A few teenaged girls might still be reading novels, their fingers twisting a strand of hair as they did so. But television sets were going off now. Husbands and wives were making their own preparations for the night. The half dozen or so passengers, sitting by themselves in the two cars, looked through the glass and wondered about the three people on the platform.

They saw a heavily made-up, middle-aged woman wearing a rose-colored knit dress mount the steps and enter the train.

Behind her came a younger woman dressed in a summer blouse and skirt who clutched a handbag. They were followed onto the train by an old man who moved slowly and who carried himself in a dignified manner. The old man had white hair and a white silk cravat, but he was without shoes. The passengers naturally assumed that the three people boarding were together; and they felt sure that whatever these people's business had been that night, it had not come to a happy conclusion. But the passengers had seen things more various than this in their lifetime. The world is filled with business of every sort, as they well knew. This still was not as bad, perhaps, as it could be. For this reason, they scarcely gave another thought to these three who moved down the aisle and took up their places—the woman and the white-haired old man next to each other, the young woman with the handbag a few seats behind. Instead, the passengers gazed out at the station and went back to thinking about their own business, those things that had engaged them before the station stop.

The conductor looked up the track. Then he glanced back in the direction the train had come from. He raised his arm and, with his lantern, signaled the engineer. This was what the engineer was waiting for. He turned a dial and pushed down on a lever. The train began to move forward. It went slowly at first, but it began to pick up speed. It moved faster until once more it sped through the dark countryside, its brilliant cars throwing light onto the roadbed.

> —Raymond Carver, "The Train." *Cathedral* (New York: Vintage Contemporaries, Reissue edition, 1988): pp. 153–156.

Mark A.C. Facknitz on Carver's Unhappy Conclusion

[Mark A.C. Facknitz is Professor of English at James Madison University and author of articles on Joseph Conrad and twentieth century fiction. Here, he demonstrates how Carver's sequel to the "Five-Forty-Eight" is consistent with a pessimistic reading of the story.]

Raymond Carver's short story "The Train" begins where John Cheever's "The Five-Forty-Eight" leaves off, just after the young woman with a history of mental illness terrorizes the man who has misled and hurt her by holding him at gunpoint. As soon as he falls forward into the coal, the young woman realizes that she has done all she should, and she says, "Now I can wash my hands of you, I can wash my hands of all this, because you see there is some kindness, some saneness in me that I can find and use."[1] In asserting herself in this way, Miss Dent makes herself whole and human, and whether the man is profoundly changed, or merely profoundly shaken, matters little for her triumph provides sufficient closure. Yet "The Five-Forty-Eight" shows us that we must hold each other at gunpoint to say what must be said, and even then we must content ourselves with speaking, for there is no guarantee of understanding. Carver's "The Train" offers an even more pessimistic moral.

Details don't jive in the two versions. Cheever's man lies in coal, and Carver's picks at leaves and digs his fingers into dirt. Cheever has the woman speak at length. Instead of being able to listen to Miss Dent, Carver's readers hear her say only "be still," words that don't appear in Cheever's text, and otherwise get flatly stated generalities: "She pointed the revolver at him and told him things about himself," or "when she had said all she could think of to say to him, she put her foot on the back of his head and pushed his face into the dirt."[2] In short, Carver's Miss Dent is a markedly different person, less particularized, less plausible, and much closer to real violence than Cheever's recuperating victim. Such discrepancies between the two characterizations reveal Carver's decision to muddle her motives, and to place her near the predictable extreme of our culture, murderous violence. Finally, in reading "The Train" we cannot answer the most basic questions. Why did she point the revolver at the man? Who was he? Why is she calm?

For readers familiar with Carver's work, it is no surprise that meaning occurs other than here and now. No sooner do his characters attempt significant action than they are again set wandering in confusion, and so Miss Dent goes into the station and sits down to wait for a train back to New York as if she had just done the most ordinary thing in the world. In come an old man and a middle-aged woman. We eavesdrop, but learn little. In fact, the more they say, the less we know. Why is the man in his socks? What is all this about a trip to the North Pole? What has unsettled them? Indeed, what is happening now, and what is their relation to each other? No answers emerge, though the growing, inchoate set of questions suggests many meaningful and intriguing stories, none of which can cohere unless Miss Dent asks for elaboration, for sense.

She comes close to making contact. For a moment she thinks of telling them that that evening she nearly killed a man and even now has a gun in her handbag. She could offer her own story, and the self it embodies, as exciting and immediate, and surely the pair would demand more, for they are loquacious and would not let a gun go unexplained. But a train pulls into the station and a point of view that has stayed narrowly with Miss Dent is exchanged for one that is anonymous and broad:

> The few passengers in the cars looked out through the glass and thought it strange to find people on the platform making ready to board a train at this time of night. What business could have taken them out? This was the hour when people should be thinking of going to bed. The kitchens in the houses up on the hills behind the station were clean and orderly; the dishwashers had long ago finished their cycle, all things were in their places. Night-lights burned in children's bedrooms. A few teenaged girls might still be reading novels, their fingers twisting a strand of hair as they did so. But television sets were going off now. Husbands and wives were making their own preparations for the night. The half-dozen or so passengers, sitting by themselves in the two cars, looked through the glass and wondered about the three people on the platforms.[3]

Thus the riders in the train assume they are surrounded by a banal, safe, and stultifying order, they are alienated by an idea of order implied by the suburb they presume inhabited by people antithetical to them, for after all they are people going the wrong way at the wrong time. However, even as outsiders they think in tedious abstractions. They can see that the three are not happy and that something has happened, but they look no further, content that they have "seen things more various than this in their life-time"[4] and blandly return to their own business. "The Train" illustrates the estrangement we suffer because we assume that the inner lives of others have come to resemble the suburb of pointless order from which they issue. It tells us about people rich in incident and feeling who are only lethargically aware that the world is diverse and "filled with business of every sort," and who cling to the prejudice that they do not care to know more. They can't be shouted at. Worst of all, Carver complains, they don't ask for stories, and will not learn that Miss Dent has a gun in her bag, and that evening she did something very important.

NOTES

1. John Cheever, "The Five-Forty-Eight," *The Stories of John Cheever* (New York: Alfred A. Knopf, 1978), p. 217.

2. Raymond Carver, "The Train" originally published in *Antaeus* 49/50 (1983) and collected in *Cathedral* (New York: Alfred A. Knopf, 1983). p. 147.

3. "The Train," pp. 154–155.

4. "The Train," p. 155.

—Mark A. C. Facknitz, "Missing the Train: Raymond Carver's Sequel to John Cheever's 'The Five-Forty-Eight,'" *Studies in Short Fiction* 22 (Winter 1985): pp. 345–47.

PATRICK MEANOR ON SADISM

[In the following excerpt, Meanor demonstrates why Blake is the most villainous of Cheever's creations, a sociopath who acts on his intellect only.]

"The Five-Forty-Eight" is Cheever's most brilliant treatment of the theme of manipulation and victimization. The icy and detached Mr. Blake has absolutely no "natural" feeling for others, especially for pathetic, wounded souls such as Miss Dent, a name that symbolizes her damaged emotional condition. As a business executive in Manhattan, he hires a nearly unemployable Miss Dent to work in his office. She performs well and expresses her gratitude by giving him little gifts. Finally, she gives herself to him because she is lonely and feels genuine affection for Mr. Blake, who has given her work and sexual attention. He, on the other hand, uses her solely to satisfy his libidinous desires; Cheever's description of the post-love-making scene reveals the soul of a heartless machine: "When he put his clothes on again, an hour or so later, she was weeping. He felt too contented and warm and sleepy to worry much about her tears ... The next day, he did what he felt was the only sensible thing. When she went out for lunch, he called personnel and asked them to fire her" (*SJC*, 239). She came to the office a few days later, but Blake instructed his secretary not to let her in.

As the story opens, Miss Dent is again trying to see Mr. Blake. She eventually catches up with him as he boards the "Five-Forty-Eight" on his way home to Shady Hill; she sits next to him and calmly presses a gun to his ribs. Though Mr. Blake knows that Miss Dent could easily kill him, he is so socially conscious that he cannot call out for help. And of the many Shady Hill neighbors he spots on the train, he is not close enough to any of them to feel they would be willing to come to his aid. The narrative concludes as Miss Dent takes him behind the facade of the train station of Shady Hill and forces him, under the threat of death, to grovel in the dirt before her. She apparently feels that she has had her revenge.

Though the story is about cruelty and revenge, it is essentially a character study of Mr. Blake as a soulless automaton, one of Cheever's most revolting sociopaths, with the possible exception of Dr. Cameron of *The Wapshot Scandal*. The ironic use of the name Blake adds to the story's "heart-versus-head" theme. William Blake, the great transitional poet between the Age of Reason and the Age of Romanticism in English poetry, could not be further from the bloodless rationalist in this story. And, in fact, the gift that Miss Dent brings to Mr. Blake is a rose, which he drops into a waste basket because "Mr. Blake doesn't like roses" (*SJC*, 238). Certainly one of William Blake's most famous and enigmatic poems is "The Sick Rose," an apt symbol of the corrupting powers of rationalism embodied in the dark satanic mills of British industrialism that destroyed the poor, the vulnerable, and the disenfranchised of nineteenth-century England. Of course, Miss Dent possesses all of the same qualities.

What makes Cheever's Blake so despicable is that he responds most emotionally to women who are vulnerable and easily victimized. His reasons for choosing Miss Dent were: "Her diffidence, the feeling of deprivation in her point of view, promised to protect him from any consequences. Most of the many women he had known had been picked for their lack of self-esteem" (*SJC*, 238). Cheever's Mr. Blake becomes, then, a demonic version of the visionary English poet whose primary purpose was to release people from the dehumanizing forces of mechanization. Cheever's Blake devises his own marriage of heaven and hell by transforming Miss Dent's heaven into her worst hell, while his heaven consists of brutalizing the many women in his life and making their lives a living hell. One of the ways he punishes his pathetic wife, Louise, when she doesn't have his dinner waiting for him, is to circle a date two weeks hence on the calendar when he will resume speaking to her. And though Louise weeps and protests his sadistic threat, he keeps his promise. His circling of the date and his pitiless refusal to deal with her on a human level subtly alludes to those creatures at the bottom of Dante's frozen ninth circle of the *Inferno* who are punished for the premeditated, rationalistic atrocities they committed against their defenseless victims.

Another Blakean allusion that ironically juxtaposes Mr. Blake to the poet Blake is the letter Miss Dent makes him read, which contains one of William Blake's recurring themes: "they say that human love leads us to divine love, but is this true?" (*SJC*, 244). And one of the first statements Miss Dent makes to Mr. Blake on the train is to quote the *Book of Job*. "'Where shall wisdom be found' it says. 'Where is the place of understanding?'" (*SJC*, 243). Those familiar with William Blake will recall that *The Book of Job* and Dante's *Divine Comedy* were seminal influences on his imagination, both as a poet and as an engraver. His illustrations for both masterpieces attest to the deep regard he held for them. Cheever's modern parable of heartless manipulation and the withholding of love resonates with biblical, Dantean, and Blakean themes showing that his stories are more than simply social criticisms of the American cultural wasteland. Indeed, these venerable allusions reintroduce within a demythologized context questions that have become the central existential concerns of the twentieth century: what are wisdom and understanding, human and divine love? Raymond Carver was so moved by this story that he wrote a sequel to it, called "The Train," and dedicated it to John Cheever.

> —Patrick Meanor, "Ovid in Ossining." *John Cheever Revisited* (New York: Random House, 1988): 92–94.

"The Country Husband"

A family man who commutes to New York for work each day, Francis Weed is a dreamer who realizes he wants nothing more than to break free of the suburban inertia of his Shady Hill neighborhood. His story, "The Country Husband," will prove to be a quintessential Shady Hill tale—it is not about adventure; rather it is about adventure's thwarting. Weed may want to love, to conquer, and if he can find a quest, to pursue it even if it ends in tragedy, but his aspirations of action are denied at every turn. In many ways, "The Country Husband" echoes Cervantes's *Don Quixote*, for it is a saga propelled by anticlimax, with Weed as the idiot who fancies himself the hero. If "The Country Husband" is one of Cheever's most adept stories, it is also one of his most difficult, because the action continually ebbs away before it can culminate. It is a sloping, subtle read, one that can leave the reader with a gentle sense of puzzlement, and one, like its protagonist, that is easy to overlook.

When Weed is introduced to us, he is literally falling out of the sky. His airplane begins to flounder and rock and the stewardess announces that they are forced to make an emergency landing. Strangers confess their dreams to each other, children cry, men drink, the pilot sings to himself "I've got sixpence, jolly jolly sixpence" while everywhere, in Cheever's words, there is the lurking "Angel of Death." But the plane lands with a thump in a meadow and nothing happens. Out of danger, and somewhat embarassed, they return to their original civility; via taxi and train, Francis Weed is able to catch the same commuter line that he usually takes home to Shady Hill. No one—including friend and fellow commuter Trace Bearden—is interested in hearing about his brush with mortality.

For when Weed returns, the hurly-burly of his household no longer has any meaning for him—not squabbling children nor the painstakingly set table nor the everyday inticing aroma of dinner. Like Bearden, neither his children nor wife want to hear about his day. So Frances—who, as his name "Weed" indicates, is a not particualrly welcome member in this community—tries to sabotage this life he knows. In many ways, it is in an effort to re-create that earlier fall from the sky, for in surviving it the first time, he was denied heroic status. Like Icarus, he wants to fly towards the sun and be consumed. There is some encouragement over cocktails the next evening, when Weed recognizes the maid of their hosts, the Facquarsons, as the young woman in post-war (World War II) Normandy who was stripped and shaved bald for having invited a German officer to bed. Francis had been in the army at this time, and he is reminded of his bygone, soldier days. Bolstered by this, he comes home and is entranced and amazed to see, not the elderly woman they usually employ as a babysitter, but a sobbing young beauty by the name of Anne Murchison. Predictably, Francis Weed falls in love. Anne Murchison is perfection, especially because he first meets her in tears. Here is his distressed damsel; he takes her in his arms, holds her hand as he escorts her to her alcoholic father, and is rewarded by a kiss at the front door.

The next evening, waiting on the commuter platform, Weed spots a naked, luminous woman in a passing train combing her hair, a vision of unself-conscious loveliness that, for knights in fairy tales, are goddesses and divine signs. Suddenly the day brims with marvelous vigor:

> He was grateful for the girl for this bracing sensation of independence … The sky shone like enamel. Even the smell of ink from his morning paper honed his appetite for life, and the world that was spread out around him was plainly a paradise.

Her light inspires Weed into a crusade for honesty, a fight for a man's right to "scratch where he itched." The social niceties of his former life no longer motivate him. When his neighbor Mrs. Wrightson engages him in a conversation about her curtains he tells her, "Paint them black on the inside and shut up." In this insult, there is glory, for he is shaking off the twilight of middle-aged manners, pledging his allegiance to "Venus combing and combing" rather than to his neighbors' decorating concerns.

Back in the city, he buys a bracelet for Anne Murchison and writes her a love note. He comes home to find Anne in the hallway and takes her into his arms and kisses her.

Unfortunately, his actions, so apparently bold, have the most disappointing consequences. Perhaps it would be better if his wife Julia had discovered Anne Murchison in his arms. That at least would be drama, with Weed playing the coveted part as the rogue seducer. What unfolds is merely dreary: they are discovered by Gertrude, an unwelcome neighborhood child who prefers spending time pestering her neighbors over staying at home. Hastily, they pull away from each other and soon after, Francis and Julia depart. When they return from their party (where, the entire evening, Francis has been lustfully planning his rendevous with Anne), Francis is disappointed to find she has already left. The next day, it is revealed that Anne Murchison is engaged to a mousy eighteen year old by the name of Clayton Thomas. In the meantime, Julia becomes upset that due to Francis's earlier insult to Mrs. Wrightson, the Weeds are the only couple in Shady Hill not invited to the Wrightson's anniversary party. The Weeds fight, Julia threatens to leave but (again anticlimactically) changes her mind. Julia's bitter comments are a thrust "hilt-deep into this chink of his armor"— for the knight's garb he donned earlier has been exposed as tissue thin. Eventually, Francis Weed's angst is stabilized by his secretary's psychotherapist—a man by the name of Dr. Herzog, who recommends woodworking. In the "holy smell of new wood," Francis is able to convince himself that living his ordinary life is a quest in itself.

As a great figure, Weed is laughable; his perceived triumphs— alternating between attempts to "give the evening a turn to the light" and attempts at self-destruction—are stifled by the negligibility of his life and always end anticlimatically. At first he thinks that Anne Murchison will be his saving, for it is she who coaxes out the qualities in him that are most male. He is the wooer—buying an inordinately expensive bracelet, writing mundane love letters, dreaming of sailing away together to an artist loft in Paris. He is also the pillager with his fantasies of drinking and then raping her. In the end, the palaces inspired by his dream-girl are confounded, not by her direct rejection of him—that, at least would be dramatic—but by Clayton, who is not only young, but pimply, didactic, and pretentious. Confronting a milquetoast like Clayton is out of the question, so whereas the knights and warriors that Weed aspires to would have demanded satisfaction, Weed resorts to the petty tactic of badmouthing his rival to a colleague.

Ultimately, Weed fails even to destroy his marriage. Julia, his wife—pretty, intelligent, serene, and colorless—is in many ways the greatest enemy for Weed's longings, because she made the act of disregarding into an art. As her children fight, she "lights the six candles in this vale of tears." He wants to open his eyes, while she has created a life in which one turns away. When Francis finally provokes her into a fight, she goes upstairs to pack her things in a manner that is "composed," not even bothering to "slam the door." Moreover, when he follows her, the argument disintegrates into a heartbreaking silliness; she sobs, not about the death of love, but about dirty socks and wedding guests and insurance policies. If Francis Weed had hopes for a conflagtion, they are dashed, leaving him with a mundane muddle. So he relents, and so does she. Still, this is not reconciliation, as Francis hopes for an instant it might be when he takes her into his arms. Rather, as Julia's response—"I'd better stay and take care of you a little longer"—demonstrates, it is an act of passivity and resignation.

The scene at Dr. Herzog's office is Francis Weed's last stand. For a moment, there is hope that Weed's longing for drama will finally be fulfilled, because as he enters, he is immediately slammed against the wall by the police. Again, rationality intrudes, and Weed is again recognized as harmless. The fact that he is rescued by the psychiatrist only enhances the pathetic nature of the interchange, for it is a profession for which Cheever is not shy in expressing his contempt. Julia, in her most hilarious moment, accuses Francis of cruel acts engendered by his subconscious, "I mean the way you leave your dirty clothes to express your subconscious hatred of me." In the end, therapy saves Francis Weed by quenching his aspiration for greatness. For what his eyes see, readjusted to Shady Hill's haze, is grand.

There are the Babcocks frolicking naked in their garden, there is the "night where kings in golden suits ride elephants over mountains"—once again, Francis Weed sees the myth in his confined universe. His near-brush with death brought him close to the temptation of truly great dreams, but now this restlessness is cured. Once again, parties and children and laundry take precedence. And if the readers feel disappointment in Weed's failure to live out himself, they feel joy in the sight of the neighbor's dog Jupiter bounding across the lawn with an evening slipper and the sound of Gertrude being urged to go home. These everyday images are strong enough to endure. Meanwhile, the antihero Francis Weed already has an heir in his son Toby, whose thumps we hear as the action fades as he dons a super hero outfit and flies the short distance from the bed to the floor.

"The Country Husband"

Francis Weed is a Shady Hill businessman whose faith in his comfortable yet humdrum existence is shaken when the plane he is traveling in nearly crashes. Evident in Weed's character is a lack of charisma—he is unable to engage anyone in conversation, even when he has had a near brush with death. Even the name Weed suggests a man who is pallid and uninteresting. The opening incident, however, sparks a chain of events that eventually lead Francis Weed to a near breakdown. For Weed is no longer content in being just a man, he wants to be a hero, to experience drama, beauty, truth, and love.

Julia Weed, after her years of marriage with Francis, is pretty and faded. Her life is one committed to suburban ideals—putting perfect suppers on the table, being friendly with the most influential neighbors. Above all, Julia is committed to parties and is only satisfied when her mailbox is full of invitations. It is only when Francis snubs the important Mrs. Wrightson that Julia becomes angry enough to leave him. In many ways, Julia is the most threatening enemy to Francis Weed's quest, for she represents mediocrity and delusion. The children fight, her husband almost dies, and she turns her faded face away from discord. In Julia's world, honesty and enlightenment have no part; her children and her social engagements are her rewards.

Teenage **Anne Murchison** babysits the Weed children. She is beautiful and also distressed, for her father is an alcoholic who accuses her of loose behavior. It is she who becomes Francis Weed's idealized lady love. He buys her a bracelet, writes her love letters, and kisses her passionately in the hallway of his house.

Clayton Thomas lost his father in the war, and since his mother is not particularly well off, his family is generally considered to be the charity case of Shady Hill. He is a pretentious boy who distains Shady Hill's frivolity, is moving to New York City to work with the intent, someday, of studying theology. He is also engaged to Anne Murchison, with whom he shares a love of children, close-set eyebrows, and an allergy to tomatoes.

Jupiter is a large German shepherd who enjoys taunting cats, ripping up the neighbors' gardens, and inspiring general chaos. It is generally acknowledged that Jupiter eventually will find himself shot. His role is but a minor one, and yet it is significant, for Jupiter is a warrior who lives by his own code, exactly the kind of character that Francis Weed will never be.

Gertrude Flannery, like Jupiter, is a town oddity, a figure that inspires discomfort in the neighborhood in which she lives. Despite her loving and comfortable home, Gertrude insists on playing the role of the town stray. Her clothes are shabby despite her mother's efforts to dress her warmly, and she wanders about from house to house even though she has one of her own. "Go home, Gertrude," is the chorus that accompanies her. Along with Jupiter, she is a Shady Hill hero, for she refuses to compromise her quests for comfort and convention.

The maid at the Facquarsons is a young woman from Normandy. Francis Weed remembers her from when his soldiering days at the end of World War II, when she was shaved and stripped naked for having an affair with a German commandant. She is signficant for Francis because she is the one living embodiment of his wartime past, the memories of which have been annihilated by his life at Shady Hill.

"The Country Husband"

[One of the twentieth century's most respected critics and cultural historians, Alfred Kazin held visiting professorships at Harvard, Berkeley and Cambridge, among others. He was author of *On Native Grounds*, *An American Procession*, and *God and the American Writer*. Here, he discusses how Cheever's desperate light-heartedness, or in his words "marvelous brightness," lends poignance to Francis Weed's angst.]

Acting out one's loneliness, one's death wish—any sudden eccentricity embarrassing everybody in the neighborhood—these make for situation comedy. Life is turning one's "normal" self inside out at a party. The subject of Cheever's stories is regularly a situation that betrays the basic "unreality" of some character's life. It is a trying-out of freedom in the shape of the extreme, the unmentionable. Crossing the social line is one aspect of comedy, and Cheever demonstrates it by giving a social shape to the most insubstantial and private longings. Loneliness is the dirty little secret, a personal drive so urgent and confusing that it comes out a vice. But the pathetic escapade never lasts very long. We are not at home here, says Cheever. But there is no other place for us to feel that we are not at home.

In these terms the short story becomes not the compression of an actual defeat but the anecdote of a temporary crisis. The crisis is the trying-out of sin, escape, the abyss, and is described by Cheever with radiant attention: *there* is the only new world his characters ever reach.

> ... They flew into a white cloud of such density that it reflected the exhaust fires. The color of the cloud darkened to gray, and the plane began to rock.... The stewardess announced that they were going to make an

emergency landing. All but the children saw in their minds the spreading wings of the Angel of Death. The pilot could be heard singing faintly, "I've got sixpence, jolly jolly six-pence. I've got sixpence to last me all my life...."

The "country husband" in this most brilliant of Cheever's stories returns home to find that his brush with death is not of the slightest interest to his family, so he falls in love with the baby sitter. He does not get very far with the baby sitter, so he goes to a therapist who prescribes woodworking. The story ends derisively on the brainwashed husband who will no longer stray from home.

But who cares about this fellow? It is Cheever's clever, showy handling of the husband's "craziness," sentence-by-sentence, that engages us. Each sentence is a miniature of Cheever's narrative style, and each sentence makes the point that Cheever is mastering his material, and comes back to the mystery of why, in this half-finished civilization, this most prosperous, equitable, and accomplished world, everyone should seem so disappointed. So there is no mastery in Cheever's story except Cheever's. It is Cheever one watches in the story, Cheever who moves us, literally, by the shape of his effort in every line, by the significance he gives to every inflection, and finally by the cruel lucidity he brings to this most prosperous, equitable, and accomplished world as a breaking of the heart.

My deepest feeling about Cheever is that his marvelous brightness is an effort to cheer himself up. His is the only impressive energy in a perhaps too equitable and prosperous suburban world whose subject is internal depression, the Saturday night party, and the post-martini bitterness. Feeling alone is the air his characters breathe. Just as his characters have no feeling of achievement in their work, so they never collide with or have to fight a society which is actually America in allegory. All conflict is in the head. People just disappear, as from a party. Cheever's novels—*The Wapshot Chronicle, The Wapshot Scandal, Bullet Park*—tend to muffle his characters in meaning even more than the short stories do. Cheever is such an accomplished performer of the short story that the foreshortening of effect has become second nature with him. There is the shortest possible bridge between cause and effect. *The New Yorker* column is still the inch of ivory on which he writes. Cheever always writes about "America."

—Alfred Kazin, "O'Hara, Cheever, and Updike." *The New York Review of Books* (April 19, 1973): pp. 15–18.

ROBERT A. HIPKISS ON REFERENCES TO WAR

[Robert A. Hipkiss is Professor Emeritus at California State University, Long Beach and author of *Jack Kerouac: Prophet of the New Romanticism* and *The American Absurd: Pynchon, Vonnegut, and Barth*. Here, he points out the various battle images that run through the story, reflecting the hero's desire for violence and triumph.]

The war imagery begins with Francis Weed's fellow airplane passenger's reference to the Battle of the Marne after the plane has crash-landed in a cornfield. His attempt to develop conversation and an outlet for feelings after the life-threatening event is stifled, however, by "the suspiciousness with which many Americans regard their fellow travelers" (J. Cheever 385). Upon reaching home, Francis Weed enters a house that represents conquest in its Dutch Colonial exterior and its living room that is "divided like Gaul into three parts" (386). Francis's competitive business success has earned him his colonial estate in Shady Hill, but, like Gaul, it will be hard to preserve. His encounter with the barbarians, his children, quickly shows his own lack of sovereignty. The call to dinner, "like the war cries of Scottish chieftains" (387), increases the ferocity of the children. When his wife asks him to bring his daughter downstairs to dinner, he welcomes the chance to get away from the battle. Upset with the children's behavior at the table, he asks if they could not have their dinner earlier, only to find that Julia's "guns are loaded." He protests that he does not like coming home to a "battlefield" and finally retreats into the garden "for a cigarette and some air" (389).

At the dinner party his own experiences in World War II are brought back to him dramatically by discovering that the serving maid is the same woman who had her head shaved and her body stripped naked by French villagers because she slept with the occupying German commandant. Once again, though, a reference to the barbarism in human nature is prohibited by the unspoken demand for blind belief in the invincibility of social order and decorum. "The people in the Farquarson's living room seemed united in their tacit claim that there had been no past, no war ..." (392). These are members of the successful upper middle class of our society, and they have sought and want at all costs to believe that they have found in Shady Hill an untroubled paradise, the appropriate reward for their labor and intelligence according to the values of a properly regulated Protestant American universe.

Francis cannot help but feel that more is involved in his growing sense of isolation than the failure of communication and sexual connection between himself and his wife. It seems to him that the forces of disorder that he feels within him are also the very forces that threaten Shady Hill and civilization in general. When he insults Mrs. Wrightson by telling her to paint the inside of her curtains black, he is not only counterattacking her busybody conventionality but suggesting that Shady Hill defends itself from the bombardment of fresh emotions by a kind of wartime blackout, ironically not really foiling the enemy but using the only defense it really has, its refusal to see the light. Yet, like the brigadier in "The Brigadier and the Golf Widow," one of Cheever's later stories, although Francis may have a secret urge to see all of Shady Hill and its instinct-denying, nature-suppressing conventions blown to bits, he also recognizes that to give way to those warring impulses would be to destroy what he and the others of his class have so painstakingly created as a bulwark against the havoc that those forces can wreak. Julia makes that point so well that, unable to gainsay it, "he struck her full in the face" (403).

At the close of another party in the endless rounds of talking and sipping that Julia has scheduled them into, the host squeezes his wife and says, "She makes me feel like Hannibal crossing the

Alps" (399). She gives him the man's necessary sense of conquest, although they have been married sixteen years. Sadly, all Francis can do is dream of such feelings, for his marriage has become an empty one of household arrangement, financial support, and the need to keep up appearances in order for the Weeds not to lose their social attractiveness. At the end of the story, after Francis has begun his woodworking therapy, we are told that it is a dark night (and in Cheever darkness is often the source of mysterious creation, of images that either threaten or console), "a night where kings in golden suits ride elephants over the mountains" (410). Francis is at least free to dream of heroic conquest and sexual success. The romantic vision is his sole outlet for his frustrated, warring lust in conventional Shady Hill.

—Robert A. Hipkiss, "'The Country Husband'—A Model Cheever Achievement." *Studies in Short Fiction* 27 (Fall 1990): pp. 577-579.

LAWRENCE JAY DESSNER ON TENSION AND IRONY

[Lawrence Jay Dessner is Professor of English at the University of Toledo. He has written extensively on Victorian authors, including Eliot, the Brontë sisters, Trollope, and Hardy. In the following excerpt, he shows how both characters and objects contribute to the central gendered tension in the story.]

In an early passage that embodies the story's essential paradigm, and whose imagery is also linked, tonally and thematically, to its closing page, Weed, and/or his narrator, notice the threatened but surviving flowers at Anne's home. Hand in hand they went up a narrow walk through a front garden where dahlias, marigolds, and roses—things that had withstood the light frosts—still bloomed, and made a bittersweet smell in the night air" (332). The weather threatened, but at least for the time being, the succinct fact here, as at the opening airplane crash, is that "Nothing happened" (325–26), "things" survived. The marriage of Francis and Julia Weed survives the husband's temptation and the wife's supposed failings. Indeed, Julia never learns of the bracelet Francis bought for

Anne, and when Francis forces Anne into an embrace, her struggle is interrupted, luckily for him, by the presence of little Gertrude Flannery, whose silence Weed purchases cheaply. True to the farce tradition, no sooner does Gertrude exit than Julia's voice is heard calling Francis to come upstairs to dress for that evening's party. The marriage survives as well the argument that develops when Julia discovers that her husband has insulted Mrs. Wrightson, Shady Hill's social arbiter: "'Damn you, Francis Weed!' Julia cried, and the spit of her words struck him in the face." Francis insists on his need to express his feeling; Julia argues for discretion and vigorously describes how their lives and their children's lives would be diminished without acceptance into the social life of their community. Francis "did something then that was, after all, not so unaccountable, since her words seemed to raise up between them a wall so deadening that he gagged. He struck her full in the face. She staggered and then, a moment later, seemed composed."

Although Cheever's narrator does what he can to justify Francis's action, Julia announces she is leaving. As she packs a suitcase, tersely, Francis apologizes and assures her of his love. Julia accuses him of "subconscious" cruelty to her. She sobs. Both argue with increasing vehemence. Dissolution if not disaster seems at hand; but when she announces her departure, Francis bursts out with "Oh, my, darling, I can't let you go!" He takes her into his arms, and the threat immediately disappears. Blandly, as if suddenly awakened from a dream she has already forgotten, Julia says, "I guess I'd better stay and take care of you for a little while longer" (340–42). No motivation for Julia's shocking *volte-face* is supplied, but its suddenness, its coming at the crucial, the very last moment, the mildness of its irony, and its completeness in putting an end to the threat, allow it to be readily drawn into the farce pattern of narrowly escaped disasters. The scene displays Julia to be tied to provincial and conventional thinking, meanly vindictive, foolish, and astonishingly weak-willed, but this repetition of the story's thematic pattern suppresses any nascent sympathy for the ordeals to which she has been subjected.

—Lawrence Jay Dessner, "Gender and Structure in John Cheever's 'The Country Husband.'" *Studies in Short Fiction* 31 (Winter 1994): pp. 60–61.

"The Swimmer"

In "The Swimmer" (1964), we recognize Neddy Merrill immediately as a dapper, youthful man in his prime. He is "slender—he seemed to have the especial slenderness of youth—and while he was far from young he had slid down the banister that morning and given the bronze backside of Aphrodite a smack." He is a descendent of that distinguished line of Cheever protagonists, including the unnamed narrator of "Goodbye, My Brother" and Cash Bentley of "O Youth and Beauty!" who are fond of athletic activity, drink, and sex. Because of their cravings towards youth, their boyishness has never quite abandoned them in middle-age. They are capable of weakness, snobbery, and delusion, but such qualities also make them prone to radiant happiness. For they love beautiful days, beautiful women, and like Neddy, who has a "vague and modest idea of himself as a legendary figure" they are their own heroes. Among these men, however, Neddy Merrill will prove to be the most tragic. Naivete, or in some cases, early death, preserves these men's conceits. In "The Swimmer," Neddy literally paddles his way towards the hell that is the truth about his life.

We are not told where exactly Neddy begins, although most readers assume we are back in Shady Hill. It is a drugged, humid summer day at the Westerhazys, and the general mood is of debauched befuddlement. Neddy—after several morning post-hangover drinks—has a revelation. He will swim home, across eight miles of swimming pools, and celebrate not only the beauty of the day, but also his wife Lucinda, after whom he will name this "river." He sees his journey as an explorer might. Indeed the first part of the story is rife with enough names to make a cartographer giddy. It is a lighthearted, lyrical catalogue of the "countries" Neddy percieves before him, one that includes the Hammers and the Crosscups, the Welchers, the Lears, and the Biswangers. As Michael Byrne points out, Cheever, like Fitzgerald, has always been sensitive to the music and also their class implications,[1] and each name rings with its own exotic identity. The first leg of the journey is sunny, and Neddy is welcomed in a buzz of hospitality. But when he reaches the Levy's backyard, he finds the house is deserted. What's worse, it has begun to rain. Then Neddy experiences a graver setback— the Welchers' pool is dry, leaving a gap in the Lucinda river. It is when Neddy notices a "For Sale" sign in their front yard, less than halfway through the story, that he begins to question his memory, or more specifically, its absence. "When had he last heard from the Welchers...? It seemed only a week or so ago." Later he will say about his old mistress, "They had had an affair last week, last month, last year." Neddy, it becomes apparent, is somehow losing his sense of time (and with it, memory) as the story progresses.

In order to continue his journey after the Levy's house, Neddy must cross Route 424. In the sequestered realm of friends and neighbors, he can still think of himself as a hero, his swimming trunks an emblem of classical naked glory. This, however, is Neddy's first contact with the public. To it he appears undressed and insane, worthy of hoots and chucked beer cans. This is not half as humiliating as his dive into the public pool at Lancaster. Neddy Merrill, a fiercely snobbish man who declines invitations more than he accepts them, is forced to "contaminate himself ... in this murk" with the plebian population. What is more, he is actually chased out of the premises by the lifeguard. Neddy comforts himself with the thought of the friends ahead, but curiously enough, their reception is either bewildering or chilly. Kind Mrs. Halloran says, "Why, we heard you'd sold the house and that your poor children..." and Neddy, compelled by a subconscious urge towards self protection, leaves before she has the chance to say any more. He is amazed to realize that his friend Eric Sachs had a major operation almost three years ago. "Was he losing his memory," Cheever writes, "had his gift for concealing painful facts let him forget that he had sold his house, that his children were in trouble, and that his friend had been ill?" This will be the most fully realized of Neddy's self-questioning. For he is still among friends, and their warmth makes him feel enough of a man to bear it. After Neddy leaves the Sachses, he will be reduced to even less.

He looks forward to the Biswangers, a nouveau riche family whose invitations Neddy has repeatedly snubbed. In his desperation, Neddy resorts to his upper class status, which, as a snob, he believes will remain constant no matter what happens. The fact that he is mocked is a blow. So Neddy staggers to the pool of his former mistress—Shirley Adams—to play the final card of vanity:

> Love—sexual roughhouse, in fact—was the supreme elixir, the pain killer, the brightly colored pill that would bring the spring back into his step, the joy of life in his heart.

So confident is Neddy in his prowess that he finds himself wondering "if she was still wounded. Would she, God forbid, weep again?" This is Cheever's masterful compassion at work. In terms of self-love, Neddy is one of his worst offenders, yet his hope in Shirley Adams makes us bleed. She tells him to "grow up," adds an insulting reference to money to boot, and Neddy, upon departing, makes out in Shirley's window the figure of a man who, unlike himself, looks truly at his peak. By the time Neddy Merrill reaches his home, everything that has made him a man has been extinguished—his status, his sexuality, and even his ability to swim. "He had done what he wanted ... but he was so stupified with exhaustion that his triumph seemed vague." When he reaches the end of the driveway, he discovers what we already know, that the place not only falling out of repair ("he remembered that it had been some time since they had employed a maid or cook") and the place is empty. Like Rip Van Winkle he's lost his life to passing time and circumstance, all played out unbeknownst to himself.

"The Swimmer" is one of Cheever's most time-consuming achievements, involving as it did a hundred and fifty pages of notes and two months of work, when a story usually took him three days. One could venture that he wrote a novel and deleted the important events, leaving us with a chain of menacing, and yet convincing implications. It was also one of Cheever's most painful stories to write. "Night was falling," he told Annette

Grant in an interview, "the year was dying ... I felt dark and cold for some time after I finished that story. As a matter of fact, it's one of the last stories I wrote for a long time."[2]

Neddy's journey towards truth is one that people frequently claim they crave, but in reality, rarely do. It is in fact one of the most terrible paths; the fact that Neddy undertakes this while coasting on the backside of the Lucinda River does not bode well for the marriage. According to many critics, Neddy's path is a descent into Dante's hell from the hazy, yet safe inertia of the Elysian Fields an observation certainly justified by the changes in water, which runs from the pure sweet pale green of the Westerhazy's to the acrid fumes of the public pool to the black water of the Hallorans. There is also the changing perception of Neddy's near-nakedness. When he commences his journey, he revels in it; in fact, he thinks initially that "he would have liked to swim without trunks." By the time he does remove his trunks at the Hallorans, who usually swim in the nude, it is only out of politeness and gives him no delight. On the contrary, "the naked Hallorans ... depressed him." For as the story rushes to its inevitable conclusion, the physically glorious image of a man in his swimming trunks is replaced by another, one of a man who is stripped. Neddy's initial, stimulating bravado—common to many physically attractive Cheever characters—has turned to infernal shame. The lack of clothing is a symbol of his moral blight.

Though Neddy's journey takes but an afternoon, it is as if he swims through half a year. He begins in mid-summer, and then, at the Levy's, there is a chill in the air, and then Cheever begins to insert supernatural signs of fall. There is a maple with red and yellow leaves at the Levy's. At the Hallorans, "Leaves were falling down around him, and he smelled wood smoke on the wind." The smell of marigolds and chrysanthums—all autumn blooms—are "strong as gas." Though these are the "longest days in the year," darkness seems to come on swiftly. Eventually, Neddy looks at the night sky and thinks that he can only make out Andromeda, Cepheus, and Cassopeia, the constellations of January.

But there is even a longer time that elapses, because as Neddy swims through the seasons of the year, he is also swimming through the seasons of his own life. At the start, Neddy Merrill is a man, who, in Cheever's playful appropriation of the Shakespeare sonnet, "might have been compared to a summer's day, particularly the last hours of one." At the Hallorans he realizes that his trunks are loose and wonders if he might have lost weight. He is spiritually and physically spent. "The swim was too much for his strength, but how could he have guessed this, sliding down the banister that morning and sitting in the Westerhazy's sun?" In the beginning, Neddy Merrill scorns any man who does not dive straight into the water. But by the end, he wearily descends the steps into the pool, and by the time he reaches his own house, he is an old man, "stooped, holding on to the gateposts for support." He can actually feel his body dying, for there is a creeping cold and "the feeling that he might never be warm again." Hal Blythe and Charlie Sweet point out the fundamental kinship between Neddy and Ponce de Leon.[3] Both men are explorers, and both chase water in youth's name, only in Neddy's case, the pursuit ages him a lifetime.

"The Swimmer" offers itself to myriad interpretations, with Neddy being compared to everyone from Ponce de Leon to Jay Gatsby and most popularly to Narcissus, who dies pursuing his reflection in the water. Patrick Meanor nicely compares its ending to the end of T.S. Eliot's "The Love Song of J. Alfred Prufrock."[4] ("We have lingered in the chambers of the sea/ By sea-girls wreathed with seaweed red and brown/Till human voices wake us and we drown.") Neddy could have lingered indefinitely in the water with his phantasms, if it were not for the intrusion of those "human voices." All in all, however, the best reading is the simplest. As Cheever himself has said, "[The story] should be taken at face value. The fact that the constellations change, that the foliage changes, that all time is completely dislocated or altered in the story, ought to be taken at face value."[5] While most critics have considered the implications, "The Swimmer" chooses to leave the important facts unsaid. We do not know what has actually befallen Neddy; but it would have weakened the story if we did. As O'Hara cruelly but aptly notes, the actual details of his downfall, like Neddy himself, is "too banal for words, too deeply stained for any water to cleanse."[6]

The home, a stereotypical symbol of comfort, has always played an ambiguous role in Cheever. But in none of the stories is a homecoming more unhappy than in "The Swimmer." Truth and the home, in Neddy's universe, are inexorably intertwined, and Cheever seems suspicious of truth's virtues. His characters are happier when they are blind. Blind, they are heroes; with unveiled eyes, reality becomes a force that can drown them. Neddy Merrill enters his swim in the spirit of blind heroism—he wants to coast on a deluded river and grasp his imagined grail in a celebration of the greatness in his life that does not in fact exist. An earlier Cheever might have let him succeed, but Neddy wakens from his dream and finds himself drowning in bitter reality.

NOTES

1. Michael D. Byrne. "The River of Names in 'The Swimmer.'" *Studies in Short Fiction* 23 (1986): pp. 326–7.

2. Annette Grant, "The Art of Fiction LXII," in *Conversations with John Cheever*, ed. Scott Donaldson (Jackson: University Press of Mississipi, 1987): p. 29.

3. Hal Blythe and Charlie Sweet. "An Historial Allusion in Cheever's 'The Swimmer.'" *Studies in Short Fiction* 26 (Fall 1989).

4. Patrick Meanor. *John Cheever Revisited*. Boston: Twayne Publishers, 1995: p. 122.

5. Dana Gioia, Milicent Dillon, and Michael Stillman, "A Conversation with John Cheever," in *Conversations with John Cheever*, ed. Scott Donaldson (Jackson: University Press of Mississipi, 1987): p. 63.

6. O'Hara, James E. *John Cheever: A Study of the Short Fiction*. Boston: Twayne Publishers, 1981: p. 70.

"The Swimmer"

Neddy Merrill is boyish, optimistic, athletic, and though he is full of flaws, among them unfaithfulness, banality, and snobbery, he is unaware of them. Bolstered by friends and the midsummer afternoon, he decides to swim across the county's swimming pools from the Westerhazy house in Shady Hill to his own residence in Bullet Park—the length of eight miles. As Neddy swims however, it becomes increasingly apparent that his flaws are not the only things towards which he has been blind. Apparently, as afternoon recedes into evening, Neddy ages along with it, but only when he becomes fatigued at the end of the day does he realize that he, along with his ambitions and social status, has grown old.

CRITICAL VIEWS ON

"The Swimmer"

MICHAEL D. BYRNE ON THE SYMBOLIC SIGNIFICANCE
OF NOMENCLATURE

[Michael D. Byrne has taught at Neumann College and
is the author of *Dragons & Martinis: The Skewed Realism
of John Cheever*. The following is Byrne's skillful
dissection of the names that appear in Neddy's quest, in
both their ethnic and legendary resonances.]

Like modern writers as diverse as Joyce, Fitzgerald, and
Barthelme, John Cheever found an artistic delight in lists,
specifically a list of names: "It's perfectly beautiful. You can use
an invitation list as a lyrical poem. A sort of evocation. I believe
I've used it once or twice."[1] One of Cheever's most anthologized
stories, "The Swimmer," includes a list of names representing
ports of call on Neddy Merrill's Sunday odyssey: "The only maps
and charts he had to go by were remembered or imaginary but
these were clear enough. First there were the Grahams, the
Hammers, the Lears, the Howlands, and the Crosscups. He
would cross Ditmar Street to the Bunkers and come, after a short
portage, to the Levys, the Welchers, and the public pool in
Lancaster. Then there were the Hallorans, the Sachses, the
Biswangers, Shirley Adams, the Gilmartins and the Clydes"
(604).[2] Like the famous litany of guests at Gatsby's parties,
Cheever's list is a carefully crafted narrative device, yet none of
the critical commentaries on "The Swimmer" have scrutinized it.
We do know that Cheever began the story as a novel and that, at
one point, he had accumulated 150 pages of manuscript.[3]
Obviously, the finished work underwent a radical condensation
of material. The list of names was one way Cheever provided
concise symbolic resonance to the action. In fact, the list stands
for Neddy's dilemma, writ small.

Even the most cursory attention to the names suggests that

they were not selected randomly from the Ossining telephone directory. At the Westerhazys, where everyone is trying to shake off the mental fog of a hangover, Neddy decides to travel to his home in Bullet Park "by taking a dogleg to the southwest" (603). But he will confront social and psychological violence and conflict, as "Hammers," "Crosscups" and "Bunkers" foreshadow. Like Lear, he will wander dispossessed across a landscape once friendly, now hostile, partly because he has been a "Welcher" socially, romantically and financially.

Cheever intensifies the theme of ostracism through his ethnic arrangement of the names. On the first half of the trek, Neddy Merrill (whose ancestry is English) finds full pools and hospitable neighbors (whose ancestry, English, German and one Scot speaks of long-established social position). One of them, Howland, can even claim to be a *Mayflower* descendant. At the Levys' (the halfway mark of the swim), however, the ethnic note changes, as does Neddy's reception. In this second lap, Neddy calls on two Jewish and two Irish neighbors; of these, the two neighbors who are home genuinely care for and welcome him. Playing on the second string socially, they understand nonconformity and exclusion (the Hallorans, weekend nudists, are thought to be Communists). Of the English or German neighbors in this part of the story, two have no pools and two rebuff Neddy for his casual arrogance in dropping by. The Englishman turns into Wandering Jew.

Cheever slyly links this theme of social ostracism with aquatic nomadism through the meaning of some of these surnames. Merrill is "a descendant of Muriel ('sea-bright')." Welch means "the stranger"; Lear, "the dweller by the sea." Halloran (an Irish name) is "the stranger from beyond the sea." Neddy's penultimate stop is the Clydes, whose name is shared by a long, winding river in Scotland.

The swim finished, Neddy "climbed up the ladder and wondered if he had the strength to get home. He had done what he wanted, he had swum the country, but he was so stupefied with exhaustion that his triumph seemed vague" (612). In one of his short masterworks, Cheever's triumph was anything but vague, as his river of names makes clear.

NOTES

1. Jacqueline Tavernier and R. G. Collins, "An Interview With John Cheever," *Thalia: Studies in Literary Humor*, 1 (Autumn 1978), 7.

2. John Cheever, *The Stories of John Cheever* (New York Knopf, 1978). All subsequent references to "The Swimmer" will appear parenthetically within the text.

3. Lewis Nichols, "A Visit with John Cheever," *New York Times Book Review*, 5 Jan. 1964, p. 28.

—Michael D. Byrne, "The River of Names in 'The Swimmer.'" *Studies in Short Fiction* 23 (1986): pp. 326–7.

WILLIAM RODNEY ALLEN ON PARALLELS TO F. SCOTT FITZGERALD'S *THE GREAT GATSBY*

[William Rodney Allen is a Professor of English at the Louisiana School for Math, Science, and the Arts, and the author of *Walker Percy: A Southern Wayfarer* and *Understanding Kurt Vonnegut*. In the following excerpt, he points out the similarities between the character of Jay Gatsby to that of Neddy Merrill. Both men conceive of themselves as heroes, and both are socially devalued through the passage of time.]

Perhaps the most significant parallel between "The Swimmer" and Gatsby is Neddy's and Gatsby's refusal to acknowledge the limitations on human experience imposed by time. In Ernest Becker's evocative phrase, their lives are built on the denial of death.[6] While they see themselves as boys of summer (each mentions baseball), reveling in the youthful pleasures of parties and games, neither man acts his age. As his ex-mistress chides Neddy, "Good Christ. Will you ever grow up?" (611). Similarly, Gatsby's affected English phrase "old sport" ironically applies to himself. Yet Gatsby is so intent on recovering the Daisy he loved in Louisville that he brushes aside any suggestion they both have aged and changed. When Nick offers the commonplace that "You can't repeat the past," Gatsby pounces on him: "'Can't repeat the past?' he cried incredulously. 'Why of course you can!'" (50). When he finally gets his long-awaited meeting with

Daisy at Nick's, Gatsby nervously knocks a clock off the mantle, causing Nick to reflect, "I think we all believed for a moment that it had smashed in pieces on the floor" (40). Neddy carries Gatsby's attempts to stop time to the extreme of actually forgetting he has lost his social standing, his money, and his family. As Cheever's narrative voice wonders, "Was his memory failing or had he so disciplined in it the repression of unpleasant facts that he had damaged his sense of the truth?" (607).

Cheever, like Fitzgerald, underlines the painful truth of the passage of time through changes in the weather and through the inexorable advance of the seasons. Nick picks up his story when he came east in the spring of 1922, and he ends it late in the fall. Hal Blythe and Charlie Sweet have commented on this pattern in "The Swimmer," noting that Neddy begins his swim on what is apparently a sunny midsummer day but later encounters a rainstorm, trees turning fall colors, and finally sees a "wintry gleam" on the Biswangers' pool.[7] Both Gatsby and Neddy are swimmers, but both swim out of season. Encountering the drained pool of the Welchers, Neddy finds that "this breach in his chain of water disappointed him absurdly.... no one ever drained his pool" (606). Denying time to the end, Gatsby refuses to let his gardener drain the pool to protect its pipes from the fall leaves, and so is an easy target for Wilson as he takes his last swim.

Cheever's final nod to Gatsby is unmistakable. When Neddy at last hobbles into his yard, he finds his house dark, in ill repair—in fact, abandoned. He could be looking at Gatsby's house, as Nick sees it on his last night in New York before returning to the midwest. Contemplating "that huge incoherent failure of a house once more," Nick acts as Gatsby's lone remaining servant, and only true one, by rubbing out an obscene word scraped in brick on the steps. Cheever parallels this futile gesture toward reversing the entropy of time by having Neddy numbly stare at a broken rain gutter on his house and think to himself that "it could be fixed in the morning" (612). But for Neddy, as Fitzgerald says it was for Gatsby, the morning of his life "was already behind him, somewhere back in the vast obscurity beyond the city, where the dark fields of the republic rolled on under the night" (80).

6. *The Denial of Death* (New York: The Free Press, 1973).

7. "Ironic Nature Imagery in 'The Swimmer,'" *Notes on Contemporary Literature*, 14, No. 4 (1984), 3–4.

—William Rodney Allen, "Allusions to the Great Gatsby in John Cheever's 'The Swimmer.'" *Studies in Short Fiction* 26 (Summer 1989): pp. 292–293.

HAL BLYTHE AND CHARLIE SWEET ON REFERENCES TO PONCE DE LEON

[Hal Blythe and Charles Sweet are both Professors of English at Eastern Kentucky University. Here, they point out allusions in "The Swimmer" to the journey of Ponce de Leon, for both Neddy and de Leon chase water in the hopes of finding eternal youth. The irony of "The Swimmer," however, is that Neddy's quest only serves to age him half a lifetime.]

Cheever employs an elaborated parallel between the quests of his protagonist, Neddy Merrill, and the Spanish explorer Juan Ponce de Leon in order to emphasize the story's major theme, the futility of attempts to reclaim one's youth.

In the third paragraph of the story, Cheever invites the reader to see this parallel, an allusion just beyond his protagonist's grasp: Neddy "was determinedly original and had a vague and modest idea of himself as a legendary figure."[5] What he fails to see is that his watery odyssey is an unconscious recreation of Juan Ponce de Leon's futile search for the fabled fountain of youth.

Cheever alerts the reader to this parallel with his constant references to exploration and discovery, especially at the story's beginning. Like a mariner, Neddy, sitting around the Westerhazy's pool, notices the clouds, which appear "so like a city seen from a distance—from the bow of an approaching ship" (603). As Neddy contemplates launching his journey, Cheever describes him as a typical explorer: he charts his path "with a cartographer's eye, that string of swimming pools, that quasi-subterranean stream that curved across the country. He had made a discovery, a contribution to modern geography: he would name the stream Lucinda after his wife" (603). Like the famous explorers, Neddy is preoccupied with cartography: "The only maps and charts he had to go by were remembered or imaginary, but these were clear enough" (604). Cheever further alerts the reader to the Ponce de Leon parallel by describing the direction of the journey; just as the Spanish explorer trekked southwesterly across Florida, so Neddy moves in a "southwest" (603) direction. While Neddy is not conscious of the specific historical model, he is conscious "that he was a pilgrim, an explorer, a man with a destiny" (604). He even begins to regard his friends along the way as inhabitants of newly discovered lands: "He saw then, like any explorer, that the hospitable customs and traditions of the natives would have to be handled with diplomacy if he was ever going to reach his destination" (604).

Throughout his "progress" (605), the Elizabethan term for a formal journey, Neddy Merrill encounters hazards typical of early explorers like Ponce de Leon. He shuns people, "anxious not to get caught in any conversation that would delay his voyage" (605). He weathers a storm that he, like any good mariner, knows is coming because he can identify the cloud formations. When he finds one of the waterways/pools dried up, Neddy "felt like some explorer who seeks a torrential headwater and finds a dead stream" (606). He runs into a long stretch of dry land where he must make "his most difficult portage" (607). Personal safety becomes less important than the discovery: "Why was he determined to complete his journey even if it meant putting his life in danger?" (607). The answer, he tells himself, is that "he was an explorer, a pilgrim" (608).

Cheever also draws other parallels between Juan Ponce de Leon and Neddy Merrill. As the Spanish explorer discovered Florida on a Sunday, so "The Swimmer" takes place on a Sunday. Ponce de Leon gave his discovery the Spanish name *Pascua Florida* ("flowery Sunday"); Cheever emphasizes flowers throughout the story, whether they are "flowery apple trees" (604), "roses" (604), "a dwarf with some flowers" (606), or "chrysanthemums or marigolds" (611).

The strongest evidence that Cheever's protagonist unconsciously retraces Ponce de Leon's steps, however, is Neddy Merrill's methodology. As the Spanish explorer searched for the fountain of youth, so Ned continuously immerses himself in its contemporary suburban counterpart, the swimming pool. Ironically, each of his fifteen attempts produces the opposite effect—he grows older. He starts out vital and strong, finding swimming "a natural condition" (604); he hurls himself into pools and disdains the ladder, preferring to hoist himself out. By the tenth pool, though, "his arms were lame. His legs felt rubbery and ached at the joints" (609). At the next pool he is "gasping, close to drowning" (610). By the thirteenth pool, he paddles, not swims, and uses the ladder. At the last pool he must rest and is "stupefied with exhaustion" (612).

By the end of the story, Neddy has not been able to find the rejuvenating liquid, and he even conceptualizes his search in terms of a modern Ponce de Leon. Having suffered injuries along the way, also like the Spanish explorer, he goes to the pool of his ex-mistress, hoping "they could be cured here" with "the supreme elixir" (611). In the manner of ancient mariners, he studies the stars to ascertain his position, but the constellations are out of whack. And as he stands before his empty and darkened house, he is unable to grasp what Cheever's historical motif has made clear to the reader: his search has been futile—like Ponce de Leon's, doomed to failure.

NOTES

5. *The Stories of John Cheever* (New York: Alfred A. Knopf, 1978), p. 603. Subsequent references will be indicated in the text.

—Hal Blythe and Charlie Sweet, "An Historial Allusion in Cheever's 'The Swimmer.'" *Studies in Short Fiction* 26 (Fall 1989): pp. 557–9.

NATHAN CERVO ON ALLUSIONS TO DEATH AND THE UNDERWORLD

[Nathan Cervo is Professor of English at Franklin Pierce College and has written articles on a diverse range of poets and novelists, from Yeats and Joyce to Hopkins and Melville. In the following, Cervo argues that Neddy Merrill is less a soul descending from limbo into hell than a walking ghost who comes into the awareness of his demise. Unfortunately, Cervo never makes it clear whether he believes that Merrill is a literal ghost, or merely a metaphorical one.]

Critics of John Cheever's short story "The Swimmer" have failed to perceive that Neddy Merrill, the man who decides to "swim home" by way of his neighbors' pools, is dead, an earthbound ghost. To account for Merrill's inchoate frame of mind and memory failure, critics have proposed various states of unconsciousness or semiconsciousness as in Loren C. Bell's "'The Swimmer': A Midsummer's Nightmare" (*Studies in Short Fiction* 24 [1987]: 433–36).

Thematically, Cheever suggests the fact that Merrill is dead through two main paradigms, which the attentive reader has to fill in, since Cheever proposes them as subtle, Ruskinian "fine grotesques." The first paradigm is that of the Pluto-Persephone myth, which reveals that Merrill's "home" is Hades. The story opens "at the edge of the Westerhazys' pool." The pool, we are told, has a "high iron content." From that pool Merrill extrapolates a "string of swimming pools," a "quasi-subterranean stream." Merrill starts off, and things are kept pretty much on a naturalistic or rationalistic level until he crosses the highway with "a grass divider." He proceeds to a "Recreation Center" (the home truth of his banal hedonism, in which there is no room for resurrection), which contains "a public pool." Obliged to take a shower, he "washed his feet in a cloudy and bitter solution." He remembers "the sapphire water at the Bunkers' with longing." He next proceeds to the Hallorans'. Mrs. Halloran "was reading the *Times*. Mr. Halloran was taking beech leaves out of the water with a scoop." Both are naked, and Merrill removes his trunks so that he may be naked too. The Hallorans' daughter is named Helen. When Merrill first enters the Hallorans' property, he "called hullo, hullo." Cheever tells us that the Hallorans' pool was perhaps the oldest in the county." Further, "it had no filter or pump and its waters were the opaque gold of the stream."

The Hallorans are Pluto and Persephone figures. Their pool is the Stygian pool. The *Hall* of their name is refined in the *Hel* of their only daughter's name, and also sounds like the *hull* of Merrill's initial "hullo, hullo." In short, he has entered the pagan Underworld, where, as in Virgil's *Aeneid*, the dead souls fritter about at the edge of the River Styx, some of them extending their arms "with longing" ("*cum amore*") toward the other shore. In this light, Merrill's forgetfulness is attributable to the fact that he is actually swimming in the River Lethe, the Underworld River of Forgetfulness. And it is only natural that Pluto's pool should be "opaque gold," because *Plutos* means "rich" in Greek, and Pluto is rich because he is ruler of the Underworld, the mineral kingdom, which, like the Westerhazys' pool, also has "high iron content."

The second paradigm is something of a collage, with puns and details flaring into each other. It is the suicide paradigm. We are told that Merrill's "own house stood in Bullet Park, eight miles to the south." The number *8* suggests two zeros reflecting each other, one of them "subterranean" or "to the south." The lower *0* suggests the truth that life has driven "home" to Merrill: namely, he is a financial failure, hence, less than nothing. It is chimed when Merrill arrives at his eternal "home," most prominently figured by the Hallorans' estate, and calls "hullo, hullo." Taken in connection with *8* and "to the south" (posthumation). "Bullet Park" is offered as a causative clue, the effect being Merrill's suicide. It is clear that Merrill's swim takes place out of time, because "midsummer," "wintry gleam," and "autumnal fragrance" are conflated during the course of it. It is the autumnal phase that ties in with "the night air, strong as gas": and the "gas" ties in with Merrill's going to the garage when he finally reaches his empty, blighted, and abandoned "home": "He tried the garage doors to see what cars were in but the doors were locked and rust came off the handles onto his hands." As an earthbound ghost, he simply retraces the tether that is the fitful content of his disremembered strategy of stowing his treasure on earth rather than in heaven.

—Nathan Cervo, "Cheever's 'The Swimmer.'" *Explicator* 50 (Fall 1991): pp. 49–50.

WORKS BY

John Cheever

SHORT STORY COLLECTIONS

The Way Some People Live, 1943.
The Enormous Radio and Other Stories, 1953.
The Housebreaker of Shady Hill and Other Stories, 1958.
Some People, Places, and Things that Will Not Appear in My Next Novel, 1961.
The Brigadier and the Golf Widow, 1964.
The World of Apples, 1973.
The Stories of John Cheever, 1978.
Thirteen Uncollected Stories of John Cheever, 1994.

NOVELS

The Wapshot Chronicle, 1957.
The Wapshot Scandal, 1964.
Bullet Park, 1969.
Falconer, 1977.
Oh, What a Paradise It Seems, 1982.

NONFICTION

The Journals of John Cheever, 1991.
The Letters of John Cheever, edited by Benjamin Cheever, 1988.

John Cheever

Adams, Timothy D. "'Neither out Far nor in Deep': Religion and Suburbian in the Fiction of John Cheever, John Updike, and Walker Percy." In *Literature and the Visual Arts in Contemporary Society*, edited by Suzanne Ferguson and Barbara Groselclose. Columbus: Ohio State University Press, 1985: 47–72.

Ball, Loren C. "'The Swimmer': A Midsummer's Nightmare." *Studies in Short Fiction* 24, no. 4 (1987): 433–436.

Baumgartner, M.P. *The Moral Order of A Suburb*. New York: Oxford University Press, 1988.

Blythe, Hal, and Charlie Sweet. "Cheever's Dark Knight of the Soul: The Failed Quest of Neddy Merrill." *Studies in Short Fiction* 29 (Summer 1992): 347–352.

Bosha, Francis J., ed. *The Critical Response to John Cheever. Critical Responses in Arts and Letters*, Number 6. Westport, CT: Greenwood Press, 1994.

———. *John Cheever: A Reference Guide*. Boston: G.K. Hall, 1991.

Brans, Jo. "Stories to Comprehend Life: An Interview with John Cheever." *Southwest Review* 65 (1980): 337–345.

Cheever, Susan. *Home Before Dark*. Boston: Houghton Mifflin, 1984.

Coale, Samuel. *John Cheever*. New York: Ungar, 1977.

Collins, R.G., "From Subject to Object and Back Again: Individual Identity in John Cheever's Fiction," *Twentieth Century Literature* 28 (1982): 1–13.

———, ed. *Critical Essays on John Cheever*. G.K. Hall: Boston, 1982.

Cowley, Malcolm. "John Cheever: The Novelist's Life as a Drama." *Sewanee Review* 91, no. 1 (Winter 1983): 1–16.

Donaldson, Scott, ed. *Conversations with John Cheever.* Jackson: University Press of Mississippi, 1987.

———. *John Cheever: A Biography.* New York: Random House, 1988.

Fogelman, Bruce. "A Key Pattern of Images in John Cheever's Short Fiction." *Studies in Short Fiction* 26 (1989): 463–472.

Gerlach, John. "Closure in Modern Fiction: Cheever's 'The Enormous Radio' and 'Artemis, the Honest Well-Digger.'" *Modern Fiction Studies* 28 (1982): 145–152.

Gottleib, Robert, Mary Cheever, Susan Cheever, Benjamin Cheever, and Federico Cheever, editors. *The Journals of John Cheever.* New York: Alfred A. Knopf, 1991.

———. *John Cheever: The Hobgoblin Company of Love.* Grand Rapids, MI: William B. Eerdmans, 1983.

———. "The Vision of John Cheever." *New Catholic World* 228 (1985): 174–176.

Hausdorff, Don. "Politics and Economics: The Emergence of a *The New Yorker* Tone." *Studies in American Humor* 3, no. 1 (1984): 74–82.

Meanor, Patrick. *John Cheever Revisited.* Boston: Twayne Publishers, 1995.

Morace, Robert. "From Parallels to Paradise: The Lyrical Structure of Cheever's Fiction." *Twentieth Century Literature* 35 (1989): 502–528.

O'Hara, James E. *John Cheever: A Study of the Short Fiction.* Boston: Twayne Publishers, 1981.

Reuben, Paul P. "Chapter 10: Late Twentieth Century, 1945 to the Present—John Cheever." *PAL: Perspectives in American Literature—A Research and Reference Guide.* URL: http://www.csustan.edu/english/reuben/pal/chap10/cheever.html.

Rovit, Earl. "Modernism and Three Magazines: An Editorial Revolution." *The Sewanee Review* 18, no. 4 (1985): 541–553.

Trakas, Deno. "John Cheever: An Annotated Secondary Bibliography (1943–1978)." *Resources for American Literary Study* 9 (1979): 181–99.

Waldeland, Lynne. *John Cheever.* Boston: Twayne Publishers, 1979.

Wilkinson, Claude. "John Cheever: Dodging the Bullet." *Arkansas Quarterly* 2, no. 4 (October 1993): 325–334.

ACKNOWLEDGMENTS

"What Happened," by John Cheever in *Understanding Fiction*, edited by Cleanth Brooks and Robert Penn Warren. (New York: Appelton-Century-Crofts, 1959): pp. 570–72. © 1959 by Mary Cheever. Reprinted by permission of Mary Cheever.

From *John Cheever: A Study of the Short Fiction*, by James E. O'Hara (Boston:Twayne Publishers, 1988): pp. 29–30, 31–32. © 1988 by Twayne Publishers. Reprinted by permission of The Gale Group.

John Cheever Revisited, by Patrick Meanor (New York: Random House, 1988): pp. 43–46, 52–54, 92–94. © 1988 by Random House. Reprinted by permission.

"Career/1951–1956," by Scott Donaldson. From *John Cheever: A Biography* (New York: Random House, 1988): pp. 139–141. © 1988 by Scott Donaldson. Reprinted by permission.

"Cheever's Use of Mythology in 'The Enormous Radio,'" by Burton Kendle. From *Studies in Short Fiction* 4 (Spring 1967): pp. 262–64. © 1967 by *Studies in Short Fiction, Inc.* Reprinted by permission.

"'Young Goodman Brown' and 'The Enormous Radio,'" by Henrietta Ten Harmsel. From *Studies in Short Fiction* 9 (Fall 1972): pp. 407–8. © 1972 by *Studies in Short Fiction, Inc.* Reprinted by permission.

From "Love and Usefulness: Life in Shady Hill and Elsewhere," by Lynne Waldeland. *John Cheever* (Boston: Twayne Publishers, 1979): pp. 70–71. © 1979 by The Gale Group. Reprinted by permission.

"Themes in Tension" by George W. Hunt. From *John Cheever: The Hobgoblin Company of Love*: pp. 88–89 © 1983 William B. Eardmans Publishing Company. Used by permission of the publisher.

From *Cathedral* by Raymond Carver, copyright © 1983 by Raymond Carver. Used by permission of Alfred A. Knopf, a division of Random House, Inc.

"Missing the Train: Raymond Carver's Sequel to John Cheever's 'The Five-Forty-Eight,'" by Mark A.C. Facknitz. From *Studies in Short Fiction* 22 (Winter 1985): pp. 345–47. © 1985 by *Studies in Short Fiction, Inc.* Reprinted by permission.

"O'Hara, Cheever, and Updike," by Alfred Kazin. From *The New York Review of Books*, (April 19, 1973): pp. 15–18. Reprinted with permission from *The New York Review of Books*. Copyright © 1973 NYREV, Inc.

"'The Country Husband'—A Model Cheever Achievement," by Robert A. Hipkiss. From *Studies in Short Fiction* 27 (Fall 1990): pp. 577–579. © 1990 by *Studies in Short Fiction, Inc.* Reprinted by permission.

"Gender and Structure in John Cheever's 'The Country Husband,'" by Lawrence Jay Dessner. From *Studies in Short Fiction* 31 (Winter 1994): pp. 60–61. © 1994 by *Studies in Short Fiction.* Reprinted by permission.

"The River of Names in 'The Swimmer,'" by Michael D. Byrne. From *Studies in Short Fiction* 23 (1986): pp. 326–7. © 1986 by *Studies in Short Fiction, Inc.* Reprinted by permission.

"Allusions to the Great Gatsby in John Cheever's 'The Swimmer,'" by William Rodney Allen. From *Studies in Short Fiction* 26 (Summer 1989): pp. 292–293. © 1989 by *Studies in Short Fiction, Inc.* Reprinted by permission.

"An Historial Allusion in Cheever's 'The Swimmer,'" by Hal Blythe and Charlie Sweet. From *Studies in Short Fiction* 26 (Fall 1989): pp. 557–9. © 1989 by *Studies in Short Fiction, Inc.* Reprinted by permission.

"Cheever's 'The Swimmer,'" by Nathan Cervo. From *The Explicator* 50 (Fall 1991): pp. 49–50. Reprinted with permission of the Helen Dwight Reed Educational Foundation. Published by Heldref Publications, 1319 Eighteenth St., NW, Washington, DC 20036-1802. Copyright © 1991.

INDEX OF
Themes and Ideas